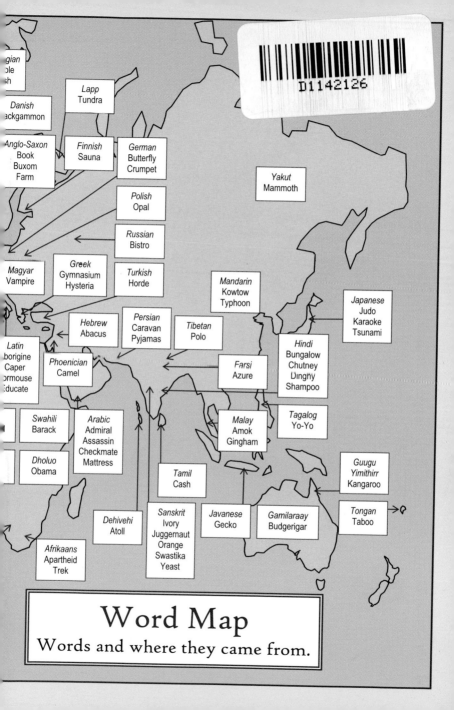

...gian
...ole
...h

Danish
...ckgammon

Anglo-Saxon
Book
Buxom
Farm

Lapp
Tundra

Finnish
Sauna

German
Butterfly
Crumpet

Polish
Opal

Russian
Bistro

Yakut
Mammoth

Magyar
Vampire

Greek
Gymnasium
Hysteria

Turkish
Horde

Mandarin
Kowtow
Typhoon

Japanese
Judo
Karaoke
Tsunami

Latin
...borigine
Caper
...ormouse
Educate

Hebrew
Abacus

Persian
Caravan
Pyjamas

Tibetan
Polo

Farsi
Azure

Hindi
Bungalow
Chutney
Dinghy
Shampoo

Phoenician
Camel

Swahili
Barack

Arabic
Admiral
Assassin
Checkmate
Mattress

Malay
Amok
Gingham

Tagalog
Yo-Yo

Dholuo
Obama

Tamil
Cash

*Guugu
Yimithirr*
Kangaroo

Dehivehi
Atoll

Sanskrit
Ivory
Juggernaut
Orange
Swastika
Yeast

Javanese
Gecko

Gamilaraay
Budgerigar

Tongan
Taboo

Afrikaans
Apartheid
Trek

Word Map
Words and where they came from.

Codswallop, Crumpet and Caper

Words and where they came from

---

by
Edward Allhusen

·OLD·
HOUSE
BOOKS

*Dedicated to all the explorers, inventors, scientists, authors
and scriveners who, over the last 1600 years, have sensitively
enhanced the dialect of a small north European tribe into the
most widely spoken language in the world.*

Jacket picture: *John Bull* by Miranda Allhusen. John Bull was created
by John Arbuthnot (1667–1735) and has come to represent all
that is best about England. He made frequent appearances in early
political cartoons upholding English decency and common sense
against troublesome foreigners; on posters he recruited servicemen
during the World War I and he represents the personification of
middle England.

Old House Books, Moretonhampstead, Devon, TQ13 8PA
01647 440707 info@OldHouseBooks.co.uk

© Edward Allhusen, 2009. Reprinted 2010 (twice)
ISBN 978 1 873590 80 5

Printed in India

Old House Books publish books and maps that help readers to explore the past.
Many are reprints of books and maps that were first produced a century or more
ago. Our guide books and maps are of interest to genealogists and local historians.
Other titles have been chosen to explore the character of life in years gone by and
are of interest to anyone who wishes to know a bit more about the lives of their
forebears; to explore their area before it was overcome by development and to
satisfy the insatiable curiosity of wordsmiths.

For details of other titles published by Old House Books please visit our website
www.OldHouseBooks.co.uk or request a catalogue.

Introduction

Samuel Johnson defined 42,773 words in his famous dictionary published in 1746 but now it is believed that there are in excess of 600,000 words in the English Language. Where did they all come from?

Before the fifth century the language spoken in Britain was mainly Celtic [*Butcher, Lukewarm*]*, but this was largely swept aside, as the Celts were pushed westwards and northwards into the mountainous regions of Wales and Scotland by the invading Angles who brought with them their Germanic language which became the foundation of the English we speak today. Since there were no dictionaries there is no way of knowing the full extent of their language, now known as Old English, but we do know that many words still in use date back to that period. [*Bishop, Daisy, Earwig*]. Over the next 500 years it developed steadily, being spoken by The Venerable Bede (although he wrote in Latin), King Alfred and other Anglo-Saxon kings. This was the age of the Viking raids and many words came to English from that source, but as the invaders eventually departed it was

* *The origins of the words in italic are defined in the text.*

3

the English language that remained, albeit with many words introduced from Scandinavia. [*Acre, Awkward, Ski*].

When the Normans invaded in 1066 they came to rule rather than to displace the existing population as the Angles had done before them and so, for a few centuries, Norman-French was the language of government while English continued to be used by the majority of the population. This language, which continued to develop largely by borrowing from the Norman-French [*Curfew, Flattery and Treachery*], became known as Middle English but it was not until three centuries after the invasion that it was used in the law courts and government. Throughout this time, despite English being the language of the subordinated population, it also acquired words from further afield for this was the age of the crusades when knights and pilgrims returning from the Holy Land brought home exotic items and ideas never before seen in the west thus introducing words that originated in China, India and Persia. [*Ivory, Oranges, Pyjamas, Satin, Sugar and Shampoo*].

Throughout the Middle Ages English acquired words gleaned from other languages during military campaigns, but it was not until the close of the Plantagenet era that an event occurred that was to mark the beginning of the standardisation of the language. William Caxton set up his printing press at Westminster in 1476 and most of the books that he produced were in English. For the first time the mass production of the printed word provided a yardstick for spelling and grammar. Shortly afterwards, with the arrival of the Tudors, the language went through more drastic changes, particularly in pronunciation. That in turn led to further modification of spellings and so Modern English was born becoming, a few years later, the language of Shakespeare and the authorised King James Version of the Bible.

This was also the dawn of the great era of exploration and travellers returning from distant lands introduced a plethora of new foods and customs for which they retained the native names. [*Anorak, Avocado, Barbeque, Hooch, Potato and Tobacco*].

As the industrial revolution gained momentum, and scientific research developed, many new words were needed to describe inventions and discoveries and invariably it was towards the Greek and Latin, in which languages these subjects had first been studied, that those who coined the new words turned. [*Anatomy, Bacteria, Factory, Inoculate, Vaccine and Vitamin*].

So we, the English, have begged, borrowed and appropriated words from all over the globe and it is this willingness of the language to accept these incomers that gives it strength, since its constant ability to adapt has been the cornerstone of its success. Consider what happened to the French language which, in terms of its everyday use, has been held back by L'Académie française, the august organisation charged with preserving its purity by discouraging such words as *Le Weekend* and *Le Email*. Had they accepted our contributions, as we have accepted theirs, one can only wonder if more international business, science and diplomacy would be conducted in their language. So, while lovers of the English language tend to sneer at Americanisms and bad usage, spare a thought that maybe you are witnessing the type of change that has strengthened it to the point at which it is now the seemingly unstoppable global language that it is.

This is not to say that the L'Académie française is not a wholly effective organisation charged with the commendable task of preserving the elegance of the French language to the eternal delight of lovers of its literature. But sadly it seems this cause is incompatible with the use of language as a means of modern communication. If a similar institution had been commissioned to stall changes in English maybe we would still be able to read *The Canterbury Tales* as Chaucer had penned it and Caxton had printed it. Perhaps also, if other languages had a similar guardian, they would not have declined or died. Consider Cornish that served an area too small to survive as anyone's first language, but thankfully not before it contributed words such as *Bludgeon* and *Puffin* to English.

Therein lies another strength of the English language, for as important as it is that approaching half a billion people have it as their first or only language, an amazing three times that many have it as their second, making it possible for a third of the world's population to converse with each other. Without this how else do Norwegians selling oil to Peruvians or Japanese buying pasta from Italians converse with each other? This is not only an international phenomenon, for many countries have a complex multi-language tradition within their own territories. Take India where the 1.1 billion people who live in the vast subcontinent have 22 official languages as well as 1,652 dialects. Hindi is the main official language but it is English that is most widely used in commerce both internationally as well as throughout the country itself. Countries do not have to be vast to share this problem. India's tiny neighbour Bhutan, which was never a British possession and has a population of only 650,000, has no fewer than 13 different languages in addition to the main one Dzongkha. But in the schools they also teach English.

So where is the English language going? Ever upwards it seems, no doubt becoming more Americanized but one hopes also now and again picking up deserving strays from the world's 6,912 known languages.

Precise word origins are often obscured because we share them with more than one language, and who knows the exact route they took to join us? Maybe previously unknown fabrics such as *Calico*, *Damask* and *Jute* from the orient travelled by camel train to Syria or Turkey where they were traded with crusaders exchanging their spoils of war for items never before seen in the west. As they returned home to all parts of Europe these eclectic participants in the holy wars; archers from England, monks from Italy and *Javelin* throwers from Spain would have taken words back to their homeland to add to their own language. Who knows if the word came direct into English from the Farsi spoken by the owner of the camel or if it went first to Spanish before wandering up through French eventually arriving in English.

Similarly it is often impossible to determine the first language the word came from since many languages are now completely forgotten, thousands more are merely dialects; there are scores of language families each with numerous members some of which share certain words and some of which do not. Mandarin, the largest first language with 850 million speakers has contributed many words [*Char, Kowtow, Typhoon*] but whether they started in Mandarin or arrived there from other Chinese languages such as Wu, Min or Cantonese, all of which are spoken by more than 50 million people, has been lost. If the original source is unclear we give the language family so that the region and perhaps the story behind the word is correctly attributed.

The peripatetic habits of words, from ancient origin to modern spell checker, have therefore been varied, unplanned and often unrecorded, but as they travelled casually through the languages of the world stopping off here, picking up a new spelling there, they invariably retained a little bit of their history and this book explains the origins of over 1,300 English words taken from over 100 other languages.

ABACUS Hebrew *Abaq* Dust.

    The predecessor of the abacus, sliding beads on a series of wires, were round pebbles laid in grooves drawn in the sand or dust. English usage of the word dates back to the fourteenth century. *See also Calculus.*

ABANDON Latin *Ab* From and *Bandum* Flag.

    If you move away from the flag you abandon the colours. The colour was the flag of the regiment that defined the rallying point on the field of battle. The ceremony of Trooping the Colour, now ceremonial, was to show the regimental flag to the troops so they could more easily locate it.

ABATTOIR French *Abattre* To strike down.

    A chilling reference to the fate of animals in a slaughterhouse.

ABBOT Syriac *Abba* Father.

ABDICATION Latin *Abdicatio* To disown.

    The act of renouncing or disowning a permanent office, such as that of a monarch, as opposed to one to which you are appointed, was previously also applied to the disinheritance of a child by someone in the permanent position of a parent.

ABORIGINE Latin *Ab* From and *Origine* Beginning.

> The term, now most associated with the early inhabitants of Australia, can correctly be applied to any people who have been somewhere since the beginning.

ABRUPT Latin *Abruptus* Broken off.

> An abrupt action invariably involves the breaking off of a situation. Rupture is from the same source.

ABSINTHE Syriac *Ab-sintha* The author of sleep.

> Absinthe is a very alcoholic, aniseed-flavoured spirit.

ABSTEMIOUS Latin *Ab* Away and *Temum* A drink strong enough to make you drunk.

> So to be abstemious is keeping away from strong drink.

ABSURD Latin *Ab* From and *Surdus* Deaf.

> The cruel allusion is to the reply given by a deaf man to a question he has not heard distinctly.

ACADEMY Greek *Academeia* was the name of an olive grove outside Athens.

> Academus, the owner of the land, was a farmer who helped Castor and Pollux search for their sister, Helen, who had been taken away by Theseus. From then on, as Athens expanded around it, the grove was protected and it was here that Plato came to hold his symposiums.

ACCOLADE Italian *Accolata* To embrace.

> Denoting the ancient ceremony of the monarch conferring accolades, such as knighthoods, by laying his arms around the new knight's neck and embracing him.

ACCOST Latin *Costa* Side, rib.

If you accost someone the chances are that you are standing at their side, next to their ribs. *See also Coast.*

ACCUMULATE Latin *Cumulus* A heap or pile.

When we say that a man has made his pile we mean that he has accumulated a fortune. A large and billowing pile of cloud is called cumulus.

ACCURATE Latin *Cura* Pains.

If you take pains your work is likely to be accurate.

ACE Latin *As* A unit.

ACRE Norse *Aker* An open field.

An acre is an area of 10 square chains and, although it can now be any area of that size, it was originally a long thin strip of open ground measuring 1 chain (66 feet) wide by 10 chains (660 feet or one furlong) long. A chain was a unit of measure invented by a clergyman Edmund Gunter (1581–1626) which consisted, quite literally, of a chain made of 100 links. A chain is 66 feet long and is now scarcely used except as the length of a cricket pitch between the wickets. *See also Furlong.*

ACROBAT Greek *Akrobates* To run on tiptoe or to climb aloft.

ACUPUNCTURE Latin *Acus* Needle and *Pungere* To prick.

ADAGIO Italian *Ad Agio* At ease.

Music to be performed slowly.

ADIEU French *A Dieu* To God.

'To God I commend you as you set out on your journey.'

ADJECTIVE Latin *Ad* To and *Jacere* To throw.

An adjective is a word that throws extra detail to a noun.

ADJUTANT Latin *Adjutans* To assist.

An adjutant is an army officer who assists his superior by completing administrative tasks. The word also refers to two types of large carrion-eating storks, although this is supposedly due to their military bearing and has nothing to do with the word's Latin root.

ADMIRAL Arabic *Amir-el bahr* Ruler of the sea.

ADVENT Latin *Ad* To and *Venio* To come.

As applied to the coming of Christ.

AFFLUENCE Latin *Affluo* To flow to.

Wealth may be said to flow to the rich.

AFRICA Latin *Afri*.

The Afri tribe occupied the ancient city of Carthage on the north African coast near present-day Tunis. They were named after Aphroi, meaning 'sea-foam', the icthyocentaur King of Lybia in ancient Greek mythology. As an icthyocentaur, or marine centaur, he was typically depicted as having the upper body of a man, horse's feet for hands and the tail of a fish instead of legs, as well as lobster-claws for horns.

AGGRAVATE Latin *Ad* To and *Gravis* Heavy.

To aggravate a trouble is to make it heavier to bear. *See also Gravity.*

AGHAST Anglo-Saxon *Gast* Ghost.

To stand aghast is to do so as though frightened by a ghost.

AGNOSTIC Greek *A* Without and *Gnomi* To know.

> The word, coined as recently as 1869 by Professor Thomas Huxley, refers to anyone who claims that without material evidence, knowledge is impossible.

AHOY Norse *Aoi*.

> The battle cry of the Vikings as they ran their galleys onto the enemy shore. Now used by people on ships to attract the attention of others rather than to intimidate them.

AIOLI Latin *Allium* Garlic and *Oleum* Oil.

> Aioli is a sauce made by mixing garlic and oil.

ALARM Norman-French *Larum* A thief.

> Bells were hung to warn of the presence of a thief. The cry went up to rouse sleepers '*A larum!*'

ALBATROSS Arabic *Al Gattas* A Pelican via Portuguese *Alcatraz* Gannet.

> These large white birds were found by early Portuguese explorers visiting Alcatraz island in San Francisco Bay and gave their name to the notorious prison there.

ALBUM Latin *Albus* White.

> An album is a book which has unprinted white pages. *See also Blank.*

ALCOHOL Arabic *Alkohl* Spirit or essence.

ALCOVE Spanish *Alcova* from Arabic *Al-Kubbah*.

> A vaulted building such as is often the shape of an alcove.

ALDERMAN Anglo-Saxon *Ealdorman* Elder man.

> An alderman is a senior member of a council or assembly. The

title of *Ealdorman* was originally used by Anglo-Saxon nobles, who governed shires. *See also Sheriff.*

ALGEBRA Arabic *Al-Jabr* Transposition.

Algebra is the branch of mathematics in which numbers are transposed into letters for the purpose of calculation.

ALIMONY Latin *Alimonia* Nourishment.

Alimony is the nourishment given to a divorced party. It does not refer to payment, as is indicated by not being spelt alimoney.

ALLIGATOR Spanish *Lagarto* Lizard.

A Spanish sailor on an English ship is said to have cried '*A lagarto*' when he saw an alligator. Being unfamiliar with the creatures the English assumed that this was the correct name for the species.

ALLSPICE Derived from the dried fruit of the Pimenta plant that grows in the Caribbean. The name of this spice is an example of over enthusiastic marketing by the early importers who claimed that it contained the flavours of all known spices when only nutmeg, cloves and cinnamon are discernable.

ALMA MATER Latin *Alma Mater* Nourishing mother.

A term of affection used by students to describe their university.

ALMANAC Either Arabic *Al* The and *Manah* A diary, or Anglo-Saxon *All Monath*.

All the months or, as is the way with word origins, very likely both.

ALOFT Norse *A* In and *Lopt* Air.

Assimilated into the English language in the twelfth century, this term also referred to heaven, atmosphere and the upper floor of a house, all of which are above us. It is also the origin of the word loft.

ALP Latin *Albus* White, a reference to the snow covered peaks or Latin *Altus* High.

ALPHABET Greek *Alpha* A and *Beta* B.
A combination of the first two letters of the Greek alphabet, *alpha* and *beta*. The Greeks took these letters from the Phoenician for ox and house which represented the first two letters of their alphabet. *See also Camel.*

ALTAR Latin *Altus* High.
A raised table positioned higher than the congregation so that they could watch sacrifices and later religious ceremonies. It has a similar root to altimeter, a device for measuring height and alto, a high voice.

ALZHEIMER'S Named after the German neurologist Alois Alzheimer 1864–1915 who first identified the disease. *See also Dementia.*

AMARETTO Italian *Amaro* Bitter.
A liqueur flavoured with bitter almonds.

AMATEUR Latin *Amator* A lover.
One who pursues an interest for love rather than for money.

AMAZON Greek *A* Lack of and *Mazos* Breast.
A reference to the supposed practice of the mythological female warriors who are reputed to have had their right breasts removed so that they could more easily draw their bow strings.

AMBASSADOR Latin *Ambactus* A slave or servant.

An ambassador is a servant of his country.

AMBIDEXTROUS Latin *Ambo* Both and *Dexter* Right.

An ambidextrous person is someone who can make skilful use of both hands whereas the majority of people can only use their right hand. *See also Awkward, Dexterity and Gawky.*

AMBITIOUS Latin *Ambio* To go round.

Alluding to the practice of ambitious Romans 'going round' to canvas votes when seeking election to high office.

AMBUSH French *En* In and *Bois* Wood.

Indicating where most ambushes occurred.

AMEN Hebrew *Amen* So be it.

AMERICA America is derived from Amerigo Vespucci (1454 −1512) a native of Florence who crossed the Atlantic shortly after Columbus and published maps upon his return to Europe arrogantly proclaiming The New World as Tierra da Amerigo. Another theory, albeit one that has not gained much support, is that Welsh fishermen had been travelling to the coast of America for centuries before Columbus and Vespucci and that the name is derived from one Richard Amerike, a Welsh merchant from Bristol who funded a voyage of exploration to Newfoundland.

AMETHYST Greek *A* Opposite to and *Methyein* To make drunk.

It was once thought that the blue gemstone was able to prevent drunkenness.

AMMONIA Named after The Temple of *Ammon* in Egypt near which ammonia was first made by burning dung from the numerous camels bringing pilgrims to worship there. *See also Ammonite.*

AMMONITE The ancient Egyptian god *Ammon* was usually depicted with ram's horns. The fossilised cephalopod is so named because it has a coiled cell structure resembling a ram's horn. *See also Ammonia.*

AMOK Malay *Amoq* Frenzied.
To rush about in a frenzied state is to run amok. The original Malay adjective referred to frenzied combat.

AMPHITHEATRE Greek *Amphi* On both sides and *Theatron* A theatre.
An amphitheatre has seats on all sides.

AMPHORA Greek *Amphi* On both sides and *Phoreus* A bearer.
An amphora is a jug that is carried by handles on both sides.

AMPUTATE Latin *Amputare* To prune.
Before its surgical use became commonplace pruning was a horticultural term.

ANACHRONISM Greek *An* Backwards and *Chronos* Time.
An anachronism is something from a time in the past.

ANARCHY Greek *An* Backwards (or against) and *Arche* Government.
Anarchy occurs when a society revolts against its government.

ANATOMY Greek *Ana* Up and *Tomnein* To cut.
Anatomy, the study of an animal's structure, is learned by dissection or cutting up.

ANECDOTE Greek *An* Not and *Ekdotos* To publish.

Anecdotes are invariably spoken and therefore not published.

ANGEL Greek *Angelos* A messenger.

ANGLE Old English *Angul* A hook.

An angle joins two parts, such as the two sides of a fish hook.

ANIMALS The English names of domestic animals are nearly all Anglo-Saxon: cat, dog, pup, horse, mare, hound, hog, sow, pig, sheep, cow, ox, bull, ram, ewe, lamb, calf, colt, foal, ass, drake, duck, cock, hen, chick and goose. The names of wild beasts, on the contrary, are mainly Norman-French: lion, tiger, elephant, leopard, panther etc. It is also interesting to note that although the names of living domestic animals are Saxon, we use Norman names for their meat: beef, mutton, veal and pork. This would suggest that, after the conquest, Saxons were retained as farmhands and thus the language retained their names for the stock they tended. When the animals became meat, however, they were consumed by the Normans who applied their own names. *See also Humble Pie.*

ANORAK Kalaallisut (a dialect of the Inuit language spoken on the western side of Greenland) *Anoraq* A seal skin hooded coat that is regularly coated with fish oil to maintain water resistance. *See also Parka.*

ANTEDILUVIAN Latin *Ante* Before and *Diluvium* Flood.

Someone or thing that is very old, perhaps even predating Noah's flood.

ANTIBIOTIC Greek *Anti* Against and *Bios* Life.

An antibiotic is a substance that acts against the life of harmful bacteria. The word was coined in 1942.

ANTIMACASSAR Oil of Macassar is a hair lotion made from coconut and palm oil that traders purchased in the Indonesian port of Macassar in the Celebes now known as Sulawesi. Much in vogue during the Victorian era and the first half of the twentieth century, it had the unfortunate tendency to rub off the back of the head onto chairs and the antimacassar, a washable cloth, often embroidered like a doily was positioned to preserve the upholstery.

ANTIPODES Greek *Anti* Opposed to and *Podos* A foot.
This word was introduced by Plato to describe the other side of the Earth, the literal translation being a reference to those who stand with feet opposite to our own. Interestingly no one from Europe had been anywhere near the other side of the world when Plato thought about this. The Antipodes Islands are 500 miles (800 kilometres) south-east of New Zealand and are so called because they are the closest land mass to the true antipodes of London which lie in the sea.

ANTISEPTIC Greek *Anti* Against and *Sepsis* Putrefaction.
The word was coined in the mid-eighteenth century.

APARTHEID Afrikaans *Apartheid* Apartness.
Apartheid can mean either separation of different races or of different sexes.

APOCRYPHAL Greek *Apo* From *Krupto* To hide.
An apocryphal story is one of such uncertain origin that the author is now quite hidden.

APPLAUD Latin *Plaudere* To clap.

APRICOT Latin *Praecoqua* Early ripening fruit.
Apricots, formerly known as Apricocks, were introduced

to Europe from Armenia at the time of Alexander the Great (356–323 BC). *See also Precocious.*

APRIL   *See Months of the Year.*

ARABLE   Latin *Arare* To plough.
Arable land is ploughable land.

ARCHIPELAGO   Greek *Archos* Chief and *Pelagos* Sea.
This is the name the Greeks gave to the Aegean, a sea that abounds with small islands and is now used to describe any group of islands.

ARCTIC   Greek *Arktikos* Bear.
The Great Bear constellation Ursa Major, otherwise known as the Plough, is always visible in the Arctic.

ARENA   Latin *Harena* Sand.
A name given by Romans to that part of an amphitheatre where gladiators fought and where Christians were thrown to the lions. It was strewn with red sand to conceal from the view of spectators any blood that might have been spilled. As such, the word should not really be used to describe an area without sand.

ARISTOCRACY   Greek *Aristos* The best and *Kratos* Power or strength.
Aristocracy therefore refers to rule by people able to show that they are the most powerful. *See also Democracy.*

ARITHMETIC   Greek *Arithmetike* To count.

ARMADILLO   Spanish *Armado* Armed.
South American animal armed with a shell-like protection.

ARMISTICE Latin *Arma* Weapons and *Statium* Stopping.

AROMA Greek *Aroma* A spice.

ARRIVE Latin *Ad* To and *Ripa* River bank.
> The allusion is to arriving by landing from a boat or ship. Riparian rights are those of the owner of the river bank such as are enjoyed by a fisherman.

ARROWROOT So called because the Arawak-speaking people of the Caribbean and the north-east coastal areas of South America applied the root of the plant to wounds inflicted by poisoned arrows. *See also Toxic.*

ARTERY Greek *Arteria* Windpipe.
> Arteries and veins are pipes that enable blood to carry 'wind' or oxygen around the body.

ARTESIAN French *Artois.*
> A town in France where Europe's first known artesian well was sunk. The Chinese had discovered centuries before that wells constructed in certain areas were able to drive water to the surface with pressure generated by the surrounding strata.

ARTICHOKE Arabic *Al-harshuf* Rough-skinned.
> The globe artichoke, a member of the thistle family, originated in north Africa where they may still be found growing in the wild. *See also Jerusalem Artichoke.*

ARTISAN Latin *Artitus* Skilled.

ASBESTOS Greek *Sbestos* Extinguished.
> Asbestos, since it does not burn, is ideal for extinguishing fires.

ASPARAGUS Latin *A* Intensive and *Sparasso* To tear.

> A reference to the strong prickles on some species of the plant that tear the hands when harvesting.

ASPIRIN Greek *A* Without and *Spiraea* The Latin name of the Meadowsweet plant.

> Acetyl-salicylic acid, which is the effective ingredient of aspirin, occurs naturally in the leaves of the plant and they have been used for medicinal purposes all over the world for centuries. But aspirin is manufactured by a chemical process that takes place without using spiraea.

ASSASSIN Arabic *Hashishiyyin* Hashish eaters.

> Members of this military and religious sect in eleventh century Persia carried out secret murders using *Hashish* or Indian Hemp as a stimulant to nerve themselves for their horrible work.

ASSET French *Assez* Sufficient.

> An asset was originally the property of a deceased person sufficient to pay his debts and legacies.

ASSIZE Latin *Ad* To and *Sedere* To sit.

> When judges conduct an assize they are said to be sitting.

ASTERISK Greek *Asteriskos* A small star. A similar root to asteroid from the Greek *Asteroeides* Star-like.

ASTHMA Greek *Asthma* To breathe with open mouth.

ASTONISH Anglo-Saxon *Stunian* to Stun or Latin *Attonitus* Thunderstruck.

ASTROLOGY Greek *Astron* Star and *Logos* Discourse.

ASTRONAUT Greek *Astron* Star and *Nautes* A sailor.
An astronaut is someone who voyages to the stars.

ASTRONOMY Greek *Astron* Star and *Nomos* Law.
Astronomy is the study of the laws of the stars.

ATHLETE Greek *Athlos* To contest.

ATMOSPHERE Greek *Atmos* Vapour and *Sphaira* A sphere.
Atmosphere is the vapour that surrounds the sphere that is the Earth.

ATOLL Dhivehi (The Maldives). An atoll is a coral reef that circles a lagoon partially or completely. Since coral reefs are organic it may be said that they are the world's largest living organisms.

ATOM Greek *A* Not *Tomos* Cutting.
This word was used in ancient Greek philosophy and then brought back in 1805 to refer to something so small that it could not be cut, let alone split.

AUCTION Latin *Auctum* To increase.
An auction is a sale where the price increases.

AUDIENCE Latin *Audire* To hear.
The word audience was originally only applicable to an audio performance such as a concert. *See also Theatre.*

AUGUST *See Months of the Year.*

AUTOCRAT Greek *Autos* Self and *Kratos* Strength and power.
An autocrat is someone who maintains power by himself.

AVAST Italian *Basta* Enough.

Avast is the nautical term for stop, as in 'That's far enough'.

AVOCADO Nahuatl (Aztec) *Ahuacatl* Testicle.

Avocados were supposed to be an aphrodisiac, however this belief was probably due more to the similarity of the avocado's shape to a giant testicle than to any proven effects. *See also Orchid.*

AWKWARD Middle English *Awk* Back-handed or left-handed, from Old Norse *Afugr* Turned the other way round.

A left-handed man was considered an awkward man since he found it awkward to do things with his right hand in the way that most people – those who were right-handed – were able to. Anything clumsily done was said to be awkwardly done, i.e. done as though with a left hand. *See also Ambidextrous, Dexterity, Gawky and Southpaw.*

AZURE Farsi *Lazvard* A place in Afghanistan where the blue stone lapis lazuli has been mined since 4000 BC.

Many other languages, notably in southern Europe, have a word similar to azure for blue, but the word blue originates from the Frankish *Blao* Shining and variations of that are used for Blue in most north European languages.

BABOON Old French *Baboue* Grimace.
The baboon has a particularly ugly face.

BACHELOR Latin *Baculum* Stick.
A bachelor was a young man training for knighthood and
before they were allowed to use real swords they perfected
their fighting skills with sticks. *See also Bacteria.*

BACKGAMMON Danish *Bakke* A tray and *Gammen* A game.
The fast moving game of counters and dice thrown into a
wooden tray was introduced to England by invading Danes.

BACON Anglo-Saxon *Boc* The beech tree.
Pigs are invariably found feeding on beech nuts, a diet that, it
was believed, produced the best bacon. *See also Book.*

BACTERIA Greek *Baktron* Staff.
When bacteria were first observed under the microscope
(*c.*1847) it was noticed that they resembled little sticks or
staffs. Some time later (*c.*1883) another form of tiny organism,
was discovered and, pursuing the same theme, these were

named bacillus from Latin *Baculus,* A rod. *Baculum* is Latin for a walking stick and *Baculine* was punishment by beating with a stick. *See also Bachelor.*

BALANCE   Latin *Bi* Two and *Lanx* A dish.
Balance scales have two dishes suspended from either end of a beam.

BALLAD   Latin *Ballare* To dance.
A ballad is a story set to music that was invariably performed with dancing. A ball, as in a dance party, has the same origin.

BALLAST   Dutch *Bag læs* Back load.
When a ship had to return home without a cargo it was necessary to load stones or other worthless weighty material as ballast to maintain the ship's stability.

BALLISTICS   Latin *Ballista* A machine used by the Roman Army to hurl stones during sieges from Greek *Ballistes* To throw.

BANJO   Kimbundu (Angola) *Manza.*
The stringed instrument travelled to the United States with slaves from Africa. Since it has a relatively straight forward construction it was a natural choice for them to make on arrival. *See also Calypso.*

BANK   Latin *Banco* A bench.
Visitors to ancient Rome were only allowed to use the local currency and had to visit money changers who set up benches where they transacted their business.

BANKRUPT   Latin *Banco* A bench and *Rotto* Broken.
In the Middle Ages it was customary for benches belonging

to insolvent money-changers to be broken up to prevent further trading.

BANTAM The name of these small chickens was taken from Bantam, formerly a major seaport of Indonesia where European sailors took poultry on board for the voyage home.

BAPTISE Greek *Baptien* To Dip.

BARACK Swahili *Barack* One who is blessed. *See also Obama.*

BARBARIAN Sanskrit *Barbara* Stammering.
An onomatopoeic word indicating babbling and incoherent speech in the same way that we say 'Blah-blah'. A term applied to the language of tribes whose speech was unintelligible to the Greeks. Someone who spoke like this was labelled a barbarian.

BARBEQUE Taíno (the language of the Bahamas) *Barbacoa* Sacred fire pit.
A traditional Caribbean method for cooking meat involved placing an entire goat into a specially dug hole in the ground and covering it with maguey leaves and coal, before setting it alight and leaving it to cook for a few hours.

BARBER Latin *Barba* Beard.

BARGE-BOARD *Verge board,* an architectural term for a decorative edge to an eave which, due to its elevated position, was clearly nothing to do with canal boats. In fact it is a corruption of verge board, that is, a board on the edge or verge of the house.

BARITONE Greek *Bary* Heavy and *Tonos* Tone.
Deep-sounding.

BARLEY SUGAR French *Brûle* Burnt and *Sucre* Sugar.
There is no barley in the sugary sweet. Barley is a corruption of *brûle*.

BARN Old English *Bern* from *Bere* Barley and *Ern* A house.
Buildings in which grain is stored.

BAROMETER Greek *Baros* Weight and *Metron* Measure.
A barometer measures atmospheric pressure, the weight of the air above it.

BARRACK Italian *Barraca* Temporary housing and Celtic *Barro* Clay, mud.
A barrack was a simple hut made of branches and mud that could be constructed to provide adequate shelter for soldiers on campaign. The word is now used for any military accommodation.

BASTARD Old French *Fils de bast* Saddlepack son.
When men were travelling abroad and thus away from their wives their saddle cloths and saddles doubled up as blankets and pillows. Therefore a liaison with a woman that resulted in the birth of an illegitimate child invariably took place on a *bast*.

BATTLEDORE, **SHUTTLECOCK** and **BADMINTON**
Provençal *Batedor* A beater or striker.
The original name of this game, Battledore and Shuttlecock, derives from the equipment required. The racquet or beater held by the players and the shuttlecock, the latter being derived from the two words Shuttle and Cock. Shuttle being something

that travels back and forth such as the shuttle on a loom, the space shuttle or trains in the channel tunnel and cock since the feathers of a shuttlecock resemble the tail feathers of a strutting cockerel. The game was played in ancient Greece but the rules of the modern sport were first defined in 1873 at Badminton in Gloucestershire, the home of the Dukes of Beaufort.

BAYONET French *Bayonne*
A French town where it is said that bayonets were either first made in 1640, or otherwise first used at the siege there in 1665. However, there is earlier mention of 'a great knife to hang at the girdle' made at Bayona, near Toledo in Spain, which was noted for 'the excellent temper of the swords made there' and this may contradict the French origins of the word.

BAZAAR Persian *Bazar* A market.

BEAR MARKET A falling market in which a trader sells shares in the hope of being able to buy them back at a lower price before payment is due. The name is derived from the story of a man who sold a bear's skin before he had caught or killed the bear. *See also Bull Market.*

BEDLAM A corruption of *Bethlehem*, the name of a religious house in London that was converted into a lunatic asylum in 1546. It has become synonymous with chaos or madness.

BEDRIDDEN Anglo-Saxon *Bed* Bed and *Rida* Rider.
One who rides on, or who is permanently carried, on a bed.

BEDSTEAD Anglo-Saxon *Stead* or *Sted* A place, as in homestead, farmstead, etc.
We also use this word when we say 'someone went in his stead (or instead of him)' meaning in place of him.

BEEFEATER This name, given to Yeoman Warders of 'Her Majesty's Royal Palace and Fortress, The Tower of London', refers to the better quality of food afforded to them over other servants. In Anglo-Saxon times the word *hláf-æta* or 'loaf eater' referred to low servants. The bread was dispensed to them by the *hlaford* 'loaf lord' and *hlæfdige* 'loaf lady' from which Lord and Lady are derived.

BEE-LINE American. Their way of saying 'in a straight line' as in 'as the crow flies' which originated in Europe. Bees and crows fly in straight lines between nests or hives and their feeding grounds.

BELFRY Norman-French *Berfroi*, from High German *Bercfrit* Tower.
Since these tall buildings often contained bells which were rung to warn of approaching enemies the English believed that the word was connected with the bells and adapted it to belfry. In fact it referred only to the tower and not, as is popularly assumed, to a place where bells are hung. So a tower without bells can still be a belfry.

BELLADONNA Italian *Bella donna* Fair Lady.
This poisonous plant was used as a cosmetic and also to dilate the pupils of the eyes, a popular cosmetic practice with all fair ladies.

BELLOWS Anglo-Saxon *Boelig* A bag.

BENEATH Old English *Neath* Under.

BEQUEATH Anglo-Saxon *Becwethan* A will or testament expressed in words.

BERSERK Icelandic *Bern* Bear and *Serkr* Coat.

A warrior clad in either wolf or bear skin who fought in a state of uncontained fury.

BETTER Persian *Behter* Better.

BEVERAGE Italian *Bevere* To drink.

BICYCLE Latin *Bi* Two and Greek *Kyklos* A circle.

So a bicycle is two circles. *See also Encyclopaedia.*

BID Anglo-Saxon *Beodan* To invite.

When we invite people to come to our house we bid them to do so. If we do not want to see them we forbid them to come.

BIGAMY Latin *Bi* Two and Greek *Gamos* Marriage.

BIGWIG In a British court the barristers and judges wear wigs. The more important you are the larger the wig. Barristers' wigs are short and kept above the ears and a senior judge has a full-bottomed wig that drops down below the shoulders. The big wig is therefore worn by the 'bigwig'.

BIKINI The Bikini Atoll in the Marshall Islands of Micronesia was chosen as an atomic bomb testing site in 1946. Accordingly, the name bikini was chosen for the newly designed minimal bathing suit because it was intended to cause a similarly explosive reaction in men. The bikini was not the first garment of its kind however, indeed they have been found illustrating ancient Greek urns dating back as far as 1400 BC.

BILLIARDS Old French *Bille* Tree trunk and *Billard* a more slender stem of wood such as a billiard cue.

BINOCULAR   Latin *Bini* Double and *Oculus* Eye.

BINT   Arabic *Bint* Daughter.

BISCUIT   Old French *Bis* Twice and *Cuit* Baked.
> A biscuit is bread that has been baked twice to harden and preserve it for the duration of long voyages.

BISHOP   Old English *Biscop* from Latin *Episcopus* Overseer.

BISTRO   Russian *Bistro* Quick.
> A restaurant where food is served quickly. The word entered the French language in 1814 via the occupying Cossacks who would shout 'Bistro!' when they wanted to be served quickly.

BLACKMAIL   Old English *Mail*
> An obsolete term for payment of money. Therefore blackmail is a black or dark and sinister demand for payment.

BLADE   Anglo-Saxon *Blæd* A leaf of grass.
> A blade can be a blade of grass or the blade of a sword due to the similarity in shape. *See also Gladiola.*

BLANCMANGE   French *Blanc* White and *Manger* Food.
> The milk dessert thickened with cornflour is simply white food.

BLANK   French *Blanc* White.
> A blank page is a white page. *See also Album.*

BLOKE   Shelta (A secret language used by Gaelic-speaking travellers) *Ploc* A broad, stubborn man.

BLUDGEON   Cornish *Blugon* Mallet.

BOBBY This slang term for policemen makes reference to Sir Robert Peel (Prime Minister 1834–1835 and 1841–1846) who introduced the first police force. At one time police were also nicknamed 'Peelers'.

BODY Anglo-Saxon *Bode* Box.
The body is a box or container for the organs. Another name given to the body by the Anglo-Saxons was *Sarvol-hus*, a house for the soul.

BOFFIN An inventor with a reputation for having a passion for his subject and noted for creating gadgets and gizmos. Named after Nicodemus Boffin a character in *Our Mutual Friend* by Charles Dickens, his last completed novel.

BOLLOCKS Old English *Beallucas* Testicles.

BOLSHEVIK Russian *Bolshevik* Majority, from *Bolshoi* Great.
Before the Russian Revolution the fledgling Communist Party split in half with Lenin leading the hard-line faction. Since they were in the majority his followers became the Bolsheviks and the softer line supporters became the *Mensheviks* Russian *Mensh* Less.

BONFIRE Middle English *Bane-fyr* Bone fire.
Animal bones were ceremonially burnt at the Celtic festival of Samhain to ward off evil spirits. This word was erroneously believed by Dr. Johnson to be derived from the French word *bon*, meaning good.

BONNET Gaelic *Bonaid* A head dress.

BONSAI Japanese *Bon* Basin or bowl and *Sai* To plant.
Bonsai is the art of growing miniature trees in shallow containers.

BOOK Anglo-Saxon *Boc* Beech.

Gothic tribes used slips of wood for writing tablets and found that the wood of the beech tree was most suitable. As slips of wood could not be rolled they were gathered together like leaves of a book. *See also Bacon and Volume.*

BOOT Spanish *Bota* Leather bag.

In Spain a *bota* was also used to describe a skin for carrying wine and this gives us the word bottle. A boot might also be described as a leather bag to contain a foot.

BOOTLEG Liquor that was sold illegally during the USA prohibition of alcohol 1920–1933. In order to transport alcohol without attracting the attention of the authorities, smugglers created bottles that were slim enough to slip into high-sided boots.

BOOTY Gothic *Botyan* To profit

Such as a soldier would do when collecting the spoils of war.

BOOZE Old English *Bousen* To drink in excess.

BOUDOIR French *Bouder* To sulk.

A boudoir, the private quarters of a lady, was originally a place where she could go to sulk and is largely attributed to the practice of the mistresses of French kings retiring to their rooms when the monarch's amorous attentions were elsewhere.

BOY Middle English *Boie* Servant, knave. *See also Girl.*

BOYCOTT Charles Boycott was an agent for a number of absentee landlords in Co. Mayo, Ireland, during the oppressive years of the nineteenth century. He acquired a reputation of dispossessing tenants who fell behind with their rent, eventually inspiring them to retaliate by uniting under a pact to have nothing to do with him – to boycott him – until he fled back to England.

BRACE Anglo-Saxon *Braceur* To bind or tie up.
A brace, such as a brace of pheasants, has come to mean two because they are usually tied together in pairs. However, it more correctly refers to the way in which they are fastened together, so three or four pheasants fastened together could also be described as a brace. We still use brace to describe a variety of fixings particularly in architecture.

BREN GUN These light machine guns take their name from the first two letters of each of the two towns in which they were originally made: Brno in Czechoslovakia and Enfield in England.

BROCADE Latin *Brocco* Small spike, referring to the awl or needle used in the production of this fabric.

BROCK Old English *Brokkos* Badger.
In *The Tale of Mr Tod* Beatrix Potter named her disagreeable badger Tommy Brock. Mr Tod was the fox and tod is a north country name for a fox.

BROGUE Gaelic *Brog* A shoe.

BRONZE Persian *Berenj* Brass. Bronze is an alloy of copper and tin whereas brass is an alloy of copper and zinc so it seems at some stage the meanings of bronze and copper became muddled. Brass is derived from the Friesian *Bres* Copper. The Friesian Islands, best known for the high yielding black-and-white milking cows, are strung out along the North Sea coast of Europe from Holland north to Denmark.

BROTHEL Middle English *Breothan* To go to ruin.

BUDDHA Sanskrit *Buddha* Awakened one.

BUDGERIGAR Gamilaraay (or one of the other Aboriginal languages of south-east Australia) *Betcherry* Good and G*ah* Eating.

BUDGET French *Bougette* A small bag.
The Chancellor of the Exchequer brings his all important budget speech to the House of Commons in a leather briefcase and invariably pauses for a photo opportunity on his doorstep holding up the small bag before doing so.

BULB Greek *Bolbos* An onion.

BULL MARKET A market in which prices are rising thus perpetuating yet more buying as traders attempt to acquire stocks at improving rates. The intense competition and frenetic activity has been compared to the fast moving and sometimes ill-considered behaviour of a herd of bulls. *See also Bear Market.*

BUMPF Slang for tedious and unimportant paperwork. A contraction of bum fodder, that is, paper for use in lavatories.

BUMPKIN Middle Dutch *Bommekijn* Little barrel.
Used in English as a term of reproach for rustics from the countryside, it was originally a derogatory allusion to the dumpiness of Dutchmen.

BUNGALOW Gujarati and Hindi *Bangla*. A low, thatched, one-storey house common in Bengal.

BUNKUM Buncombe is a town in North Carolina whose representative in Congress in 1820 was noted for delivering long, tedious speeches invariably filled with irrelevances.

BURGLAR Gaelic *Buar glacair* A cattle lifter.

BURROW Anglo-Saxon *Burgh* Stronghold, fortification.
The same word gives us borough which meant a shelter or fortress around which settlements were established. Hence also its usage to refer to the home of the humble rabbit.

BUSTLE Icelandic *Bustla* To splash with water.
The word is derived from the rapid motion produced by the bubbling of a boiling liquid such as is found in the natural hot springs in Iceland.

BUTCHER French *Boucher* and Provençal *Bochier* from Celtic *Bouc* He-goat.
The word butcher is derived from 'the slaughterer of goats'.

BUTTER Bavarian *Buttern* To shake backwards and forwards as in the making of butter in a butter churn. Alternatively, Greek *Bous* Cow and *Turos* Cheese.

BUTTERFLY German and Dutch *Butterfleige* A large moth that infests dairies and lives on butter and milk that gave its name to the entire species.

BUXOM Anglo-Saxon *Boga* A bow and *Sum* Some.
The Old English word *Boughsome* referred to someone or something that easily bent to one's will like an archer's bow, therefore buxom was originally applied to that which was obedient or pliant and letter writers often signed off with 'your buxom servant'. The transition from obedience to the

current meaning of a generously proportioned female form may be more to do with wishful thinking on the part of male admirers.

BY JINGO Basque *Jainko* God.

The term 'jingoism', meaning military blustering, derives from a patriotic, anti-Russian music hall song from the Victorian era that featured the expression 'By Jingo'. It was sung at a time when many people wanted a British fleet to sail through the Bosporus to engage with Russia.

BYE-LAW Danish, Norwegian, Old Norse *By* Town or borough.

A bye-law is therefore a local law 'of the town'. The Danes renamed many English settlements by incorporating their word for town, as is the case of Grimsby, Derby and Whitby.

CAB French *Cabrioler* To Prance or caper from Latin *Caper* Goat.
A cabriolet is a light carriage such as a hansom cab pulled by one horse and noted for being able to swiftly weave in and out of heavier traffic. *See also Caper and Taxi.*

CACOPHONY Greek *Kaktos* Bad and *Phone* A sound.
See also Telephone.

CADDY Malay *Kati* A unit of weight equivalent to 1 pound 3 ounces (600 grams).
A small packet of tea weighed one *kati*. Early travellers asked for a *kati* of tea believing it to be a packet or container of tea without realising that they were buying it by weight.

CALCULUS Latin *Calculi* Pebble.
The earliest aids to calculation were pebbles laid in rows on the ground. *See also Abacus.*

CALENDAR Latin *Calendae* The Romans called the first day of each month 'calends' which had particular significance since they marked a new moon, they were also the days on which debts had to be settled and on which important announcements were made.

CALICO A corruption of *Calicut*, the seaport on the coast of India where the unbleached, coarse woven textile originated.

CALLIGRAPHY Greek *Kallos* Beauty and *Graphein* Writing.

CALLISTHENICS Greek *Kallos* Beauty and *Sthenos* Strength. These exercises promote strength through elegant movement.

CALORIE Latin *Calor* Heat.
A calorie is the amount of heat or energy required to raise the temperature of one gram of water by 1° centigrade.

CALYPSO West African *Kaiso* Song.
Now more associated with the West Indies where the practice of singing rhythmic songs and playing on simple instruments was the only form of entertainment available to slaves after their voyage across the Atlantic. *See also Banjo.*

CAMEL Phoenician *Gamel* Camel.
The Phoenician alphabet consisted of words for key everyday items that represented different letters. *Gamel* was the third character, the previous two being the words for Ox and House. Other letters were named after Hook, Weapon, Arm, Fish, Eye, Mouth, Head and, perhaps most interestingly, Papyrus. *See also Alphabet, Library and Paper.*

CAMELLIA The beautiful flowering garden plant was introduced to Europe from Japan by a Spanish Jesuit called *Kamel*. There are over 200 species of camellia, the best known of which is the tea plant, Latin name *Camellia sinensis.*

CANCEL Latin *Cancellus* Lattice work.
Deeds were once cancelled by being marked with lines that crossed the writing in both directions forming a lattice.

CANDIDATE Latin *Candidus* White.

   It was the custom for Romans seeking to be elected to offices of state to wear white togas.

CANISTER Greek *Kanna* Cane, *Kanastron* Wicker basket and Latin *Canistrum* Basket.

   Canisters were made from woven cane.

CANNIBAL Arawak (northern South America and Caribbean) *Caniba* was the name of a human flesh eating tribe encountered by early Spanish explorers but the Europeans gave them the name Carib from which Caribbean is derived.

CANOPY Greek *Conopeum* Net and *Konops* Mosquito.

   A canopy was originally a mosquito net.

CANTER A Canterbury trot was the hurrying speed at which pilgrims travelled while on their way to pay homage at the tomb of Archbishop Thomas Becket (1118–1170) in Canterbury.

CAPER Latin *Caper* Goat.

   Meaning to skip about in a frolicsome manner, the word is an allusion to the habit that goats have of suddenly jumping about for no apparent reason. The symbol of the Zodiac sign Capricorn is a goat. *See also Cab.*

CAPSIZE Catalan *Capusa* To sink.

CAPUCHIN Latin *Caput* Head.

   A Capuchin monk wears a light brown monastic habit with a prominent hood that covers the head. A Cappuccino is a light brown drink with a prominent 'head' of foam. Capuchin monkeys have light brown colouring similar to the monk's habit and were given the name by early explorers.

CAR, CART Latin *Carra, carrum* Two-wheeled wagon. This root also gives us the words carry, carrier and carriage. Automobile derives from two Greek words *Auto* Self and *Mobilis* Moving since they were the first vehicles to move without being pulled or pushed by a separate source of power such as a man, a horse or a railway engine.

CARAFE Arabic *Gharfa* Vessel, *Gharafa* To pour and Persian Q*arabah* A large flagon.

CARAVAN Persian *Kārwān* A company of travellers journeying through a desert or other hostile region.

CARDIGAN, **BALACLAVA** and **RAGLAN**.
These three garments all had military origins. The 7th Earl of Cardigan, who led the charge of the Light Brigade, wore the woollen cardigan that later bore his name to keep out the cold during the Crimean War (1854–1856). So cold was it during the campaign that a request for woollen headgear was made and thousands of knitted garments were sent to the British army serving at Balaclava. The raglan sleeve, in which the material of the sleeve extends over the shoulder as far as the collar, was devised for Lord Raglan's coat after he had an arm amputated following an injury sustained at The Battle of Waterloo.

CARNIVAL Italian *Carne* Flesh and *Vale* Farewell.
Carnivals were festivals held just before the commencement of Lent, during which period the eating of meat was forbidden.

CAROL Old French and Breton *Carole* A circle dance.
Before becoming Christmas songs carols were accompaniment for dancers.

CARPENTER Latin *Carpentarius* A maker of wooden carriages.

CARTE BLANCHE French *Carte* Card and *Blanche* Blank.
A blank sheet of paper. Giving a man *carte blanche* means that he has no written instructions and is at liberty to act as he pleases.

CASH Tamil *Kasu*, from Sanskrit *Karsa* A weight of gold or silver.
The word cash has a variety of meanings in relation to south-east Asian currencies but the word originated in the south of India.

CAST Norse *Kasta* To throw.
If you cast a fishing line you throw it onto the water.

CASTANETS Spanish *Castana* Chestnut.
The allusion is to the cracking sound of chestnuts bursting as they are roasted being similar to the sound of castanets.

CATAMARAN Tamil *Kattu Maram* Tied wood.
A catamaran is a vessel with two hulls that are fixed together. Originally it would be constructed by tying two tree trunks together.

CATHEDRAL A *cathedra* was a chair in which Greek and Roman philosophers sat to deliver their orations. The name was then taken up by early Christian bishops and the buildings in which they installed their *cathedra* became known as cathedrals, the seat of a bishop. A bishop's diocese is also called his see, from the Latin *Sedes* A seat.

CELSIUS An alternative name for the centigrade scale that divides temperature into 100 *(centi)* grades between the freezing and boiling points of water. The first person to suggest this simple scale was Swedish Astronomer Anders Celsius (1701–1744) in 1742. The less straightforward fahrenheit scale with 32 for freezing and 212 for boiling point had been proposed three decades before by a German physicist named Daniel Fahrenheit (1686–1736).

CEMETERY Greek *Koimeterion* and Latin *Coemeterium* A sleeping place.

CENOTAPH Greek *Kenos* Empty and *Taphos* Tomb.
A cenotaph is a memorial erected to the memory of someone whose body is buried elsewhere.

CEREALS Latin *Ceres* The Roman goddess of agriculture has lent her name to corns such as wheat and barley.

CHAPEL Latin *Cappa* A cloak.
The first chapel was a sanctuary where the cloak of St Martin of Tours (316–397) was kept after he died. He is the patron saint of France.

CHAR Mandarin *Char* Tea.
Now English slang as in 'Would you like a cup of char?'.

CHARM Latin *Carmen* A song portraying grace, loveliness and beauty that leant its name to items and actions with the same qualities.

CHARWOMAN Anglo-Saxon *Cyre* To turn.
A charwoman was originally someone who would take a

turn at doing any odd job. But it was not her task to make tea. *See also Char.*

CHAUFFEUR French *Chauffer* To heat.

The boilers of early steam powered vehicles had to be heated before they could be used and the chauffeur was the person responsible for doing this. Later they also became responsible for driving the vehicles. *See also Limousine.*

CHAV Romani *Charvorse* Boy.

CHEAP Anglo-Saxon *Caepian* To buy.

An article, if well bought, was said to be a good-cheap as in a good buy. If too much had been paid for it, it was a bad-cheap or as we would now say a bad buy. Cheap is now most usually used for 'good-cheap' and the prefix 'good' has been dropped as superfluous. But its derogatory meaning is not lost and cheap can still be used in a manner unrelated to cost to describe something inferior or ill thought of, this being the successor to bad-cheap albeit with a slightly varied meaning

CHECKMATE Arabic *Shah* King and *Mata* Is dead.

The winner of a game of chess is the one who captures and kills his opponent's king.

CHEESE Anglo-Saxon *Cwysam* To squeeze.

Curds are squeezed to form cheese.

CHEMISTRY Arabic *Kimia* Something hidden.

The precursor to chemistry was alchemy, an ancient science that aimed to achieve ultimate wisdom as well as find a means of converting metals such as copper and lead into gold. Since much of the latter involved what we would now call chemistry, alchemists became chemists without forgetting that their original occupation was to find something that was hidden, most notably the still elusive process for converting other metals into gold.

CHIMPANZEE Angolan *Kivili-chimpenze* Ape.

CHIPOLATA Italian *Cipolla* Onions and *Cipollata* A dish of onions. So the small sausages we know today took their name from a quite different wholly vegetarian dish.

CHIROPODIST Greek *Cheir* Hand and *Podos* Foot.
Now only concerned with ailments of the feet, chiropodists were once also concerned with the hands.

CHIT As in a slip of paper Marathi (Central India) *Chit* A Receipt.

CHOCOLATE Nahuatl (Aztec) *Xocolli* Bitter and *Atl* Water.
The Aztecs combined the two words to form *xocolat* and have been producing it for over 3000 years. The Spanish introduced chocolate, a product of the cacao tree that grows in Central and South America, to Europe during the sixteenth century.

CHUM Armenian *Chom* To live together.

CHUTNEY Hindi *Chatni* A portion of food.

CIGAR Spanish *Cigarro*, from Mayan *Siyar* Tobacco.

CLUMSY Icelandic *Klumsa* Hands stiffened or frozen so that they are incapable of grasping anything.

COAST Latin *Costa* A rib or side. The side of a country.
The term sea-coast shows that the word coast was not originally confined to the sea margin of a country. The side of

anything may also be called its coast. For instance, there was a time when the side of a hill was called its coast. We retain a reference to that when we say 'to coast downhill' meaning to travel down the side of a hill. *See also Accost.*

COBALT German *Kobald* A devil.

Silver miners named ores of this metal after the devil before its value was discovered because it was so hard as to be almost unworkable, the hardness being attributed to the malice of the devil.

COCAINE The stimulant is made from the leaves of the *Coca* tree most commonly found in the northern parts of South America. It has no connection to the *Cacao* tree from which cocoa is obtained.

CODSWALLOP In 1870 Hiram Codd (1838–1887) patented a method of retaining the fizz in a bottle of drink by inserting a glass marble in the neck that was forced up against a rubber washer by the pressure. The slang term wallop, meaning any poor quality drink, was added to his name by his competitors who were keen to discredit him after the popularity of his device threatened their businesses. It seems they were successful as codswallop now means nonsense or rubbish. Few of his bottles have survived as children broke them to acquire the marble.

COFFEE Arabic *Qahweh* Coffee, from *Qahwat al būnn* Wine of the bean.

The word could also be related to the *Kaffa* region in Ethiopia, where coffee was grown.

COFFIN Greek *Cophinus* A basket.

In England corpses were once buried wrapped in sheets and laid in baskets but in the sixteenth century wooden coffins were introduced. The vestry minutes of St. Helens Bishopsgate on 5 March 1564 recorded 'that none shall be buried within the church unless the dead corpse be coffined in wood'.

COLUMBINE Latin *Columba* Pigeon.
It is said that when the outer petals are pulled off the columbine flower, Latin name *Aquilegia*, the remainder resembles a pigeon.

COMMITTEE Old English *Committen* To entrust.
A committee is a group of people entrusted to carry out a task.

COMRADES Spanish *Camarades* Chamber.
A military term describing men who sleep in the same *camera* or chamber.

CONCLAVE Latin *Con* Together and *Clavis* A key.
A room that can be locked such as where cardinals meet in secret to elect a new pope.

CONCUBINE Latin *Con* Together and *Cubare* To lie down.
Concubines lie down with the men they live with.

CONDOM The name of the contraceptive device is not derived from the town of the same name in south-west France but from a member of the court of King Charles II, Colonel Cundum, who introduced the device at a time when the upper classes were given to a degree of high living quite unknown in the puritan Cromwellian years that preceded their own.

CONFLICT Latin *Con* Together and *Fligere* To strike.

CONGER Icelandic *Kongr* A king.
The conger eel is the king eel.

CONGREGATE Latin *Con* Together and *Gregis* A flock.
See also Gregarious and Segregate.

CONJUGAL Latin *Con* Together and *Jugum* Yoke.
A husband and wife joined in marriage are therefore yoked together.

COOK Anglo-Saxon *Coc* Cook.
Cook is not therefore derived from the French *Cuisine*. Similarly, Kitchen is from the Anglo-Saxon *Cycene* Kitchen.

COOPER German *Küpe* Tub, barrel or vat and *Küpfer* One who makes tubs.

COPY Latin *Copia* Abundance
Creating a copy of something makes it more abundant.

CORE French *Coeur* The heart.

CORNET Latin *Corn* A horn and *Et* a diminutive.
Thus a cornet is a small horn.

COTTON Arabic *Koton* Cotton.

COUPLE Latin *Copula* from Hebrew *Kebel* Fetter, that is two items fixed together.
Thus two people who have been fixed together in marriage may be described as a couple, but an unmarried couple who are yet to tie the knot should not be.

COUPON French *Couper* To cut.
A coupon is a portion that is cut off the main article.

COWARD Norman-French *Coue* A tail.

Most animals, when running away frightened, put their tails between their legs.

COXSWAIN Scandinavian, Dutch *Kog* A boat.

A swain is a young man and thus a coxswain is a young man in charge of a boat.

CRAYON French *Craye* Chalk.

A crayon was originally a writing implement made of chalk. This also gives us the name for the River Cray which rises in the chalk hills of Surrey and runs through Croydon and Foot's Cray.

CRESCENT Latin *Crescens* To grow.

This word originally had no reference to a shape but to a moon that was growing or waxing, Frisian *Waxa* To increase, as opposed to one that was reducing or waning Norse *Wan* To Lessen.

CREW CUTS American oarsmen in university rowing eights adopted the habit of short hair in the belief that a crew with short hair met less wind resistance.

CRICKET Saxon *Crice* A staff or stick.

The ball was originally struck by a *criccette* a short staff or stick. *See also Rugby and Soccer.*

CRINOLINE Latin *Crinis* Hair.

The elaborate skirts were originally stiffened with a coarse cloth made of horse hair.

CRIPPLE Anglo-Saxon *Creopare* A creeper.

Without assistance cripples were forced to creep along the ground.

CROCHET French *Croc* A hook.

A crochet is therefore a little hook as used in this method of knitting wool and thread together.

CROCKERY Welsh *Crochan*, Manx *Crocan*, Gaelic *Crogan* Pot or Icelandic *Krukka*. All words for Earthenware pot or pitcher.

CRONE Anglo-Norman *Carogne* A ewe that has lost her teeth.

The term that is now applied to cantankerous old women was once used in a much less derogatory manner to describe women who had entered the last phase of their lives and had begun to embody the attributes of wisdom, maturity and spirituality that go with it.

CROUCH Old English *Couch* To lie down, to conceal.

A tiger crouches in long grass to conceal itself.

CROWBAR Old English *Cro* A curve.

A crowbar is a metal tool with a curve at one end designed to increase leverage.

CROWD Old English *Crudan* To press, to crush and Norwegian *Kryda* To swarm.

CRUMPET German *Krump* Bent or crumpled.

The holes on the surface of a crumpet, created by the use of extra baking powder, give an uneven or crumpled appearance.

CUPBOARD English *Cup* and Norman-French *Boor* Parlour.

A cupboard is therefore a room in which cups are kept, not a shelf behind a door.

CURFEW   Norman-French *Couvre de feu* Cover the fire.

A law enforced by William the Conqueror but previously instituted by King Alfred. The curfew bell was rung each evening when cooking fires had to be extinguished. The most famous case when this regulation was ignored was on the 1st of September 1666, when the King's baker Thomas Farynor, of Pudding Lane, went to bed without covering his fire and a spark from the oven left burning set fire to some wood stacked nearby thus starting the Great Fire of London.

CURMUDGEON   Old English *Corn mudgin* Corn trader.

Mudgins were merchants and those who traded in corn were invariably unpopular due to accusations of hoarding grain in order to keep the price up. Hence the word came to mean an avaricious monopolist. Samuel Johnson, however, when compiling his dictionary, could not find the word's derivation so he inserted a query seeking advice on the matter. An anonymous reply advised him that curmudgeon was formed by combining French *Cœur* Heart and *Méchant* Bad, thus taken literally to mean 'bad heart'. Johnson added that his explanation was from 'an unknown correspondent'.

CURRANT   Greek *Corinth* The province where the seedless grapes were first cultivated and dried.

CYNICAL   Greek *Kunikos* Dog-like.

The term first appeared in Ancient Greece as the name for a new school of philosophers who rejected wealth and power in favour of a lifestyle without possessions, in keeping with virtue and nature. They were often to be found begging on the streets of Rome from the first century AD and were thus considered wild and dog-like. Passers-by became sceptical of their motives and the word evolved to mean any person who was unconvinced by another's thinking.

CZAR, **TZAR** Latin *Caesar* To Cut and later Emperor.

So dangerous was the section operation, the cutting of the mother to give birth to the baby, that it was only performed when the mother had died. Julius Caesar could not have been born by this method since we know his mother lived long after his birth, but one of his ancestors was probably born in this way and the name Caesar became something of a family name. After Julius Caesar was succeeded by Augustus, the name became synonymous with the title of Emperor even though his successors were not of the same family. The word Czar, used to describe the supreme ruler of Russia and its sovereign states between 1547 and 1917, as well as the rulers of Bulgaria and Serbia at various times, derives from Caesar. *Kaiser*, the title given to the rulers of the Austrian, Austro-Hungarian and German Empires, between 1804 and 1918, is also from Caesar.

DAB Middle English *Dabben* To strike.

To dab was originally to deliver a heavy blow with a weapon but with time it has reduced in ferocity to no more than a gentle pat. Dab is slang for a finger print, evidence of the gentle touch of the hand.

DACHSHUND German *Dachs* Badger and *Hund* Dog.

The mummified remains of similar dogs have been found in Ancient Egyptian burial chambers but more recently they were bred in Europe to hunt badgers and rabbits. Their short legs are more to do with modern fashion than by-gone pursuit.

DAGGER Spanish *Daga* A sword.

DAIRY Old English *Dey* A farm servant, usually a female, whose duty was to make cheese and butter and attend to the calves. The *deyry* was the department under her care.

DAISY Old English *Daeges* Day and *Eage* Eye.

The daisy closes its petals at night so the 'eye' is only seen in the day.

DALLY French *Dalier* To chat.

> To dally now means to dawdle but it derives from the common practice of chatting while doing so. Dilly-dally, as in the old music hall song '*My old man said "Follow the van and don't dilly-dally on the way"*' means the same thing as dally.

DAM The *Dam* was a small Indian coin thus 'I don't care a dam' or 'I don't give a dam' is not swearing but means 'I don't care a penny'.

DAMASK This linen takes its name from Damascus in Syria, from where it was first imported to Europe by returning crusaders having been carried there by camel trains from the east. Before the name of the city at which they bought the cloth with woven designs gave its name to the material it was called Diaper as that word means a geometric pattern of alternating colours such as was often woven into the cloth. From there the word went in two directions. As a pattern, diaper is still applied to walls made of bricks of varying colours arranged into intricate designs. As a cloth it travelled across the Atlantic to America to be used to describe what in Europe is called a nappy. *See also Napkin.*

DANDELION French *Dent de Lion* Lion's tooth.

> The petals are said to resemble the teeth of a lion.

DATE (The fruit.) Greek *Daktylos* Finger.

> The slender leaves of the date palm resemble fingers.

DAYS OF THE WEEK With the exception of Saturday, the names for the days of the week are all derived from northern European sources, whereas the months of the year are all of Greek or Latin origin. *See also Months of the Year.*

Sunday: The day of the Sun, a celebration of the importance of the Sun. Most northern European languages, including the lesser known Saxon, Norse and Frisian, have a similar name for the day that was always considered the first day of the week until it was consumed by the weekend.

Monday: The day of the Moon. Before the standardisation of the calendar the moon played a far more significant role in peoples lives, indeed as long ago as the Stone Age, time was measured in moons and it is from the moon that the word month is derived.

Tuesday: Old English *Tiwes dæg* A day in honour of Tyr who was the Norse god of war, their equivalent of the Roman Mars. In other words, both Tuesday and March have similarly martial roots.

Wednesday: Old English *Wēdnes dæg* The day of Woden or Odin, the foremost god of the Norsemen who remained an important god in England until the arrival of Christianity and was god of wisdom, battles and hunting.

Thursday: Thor's day. Thor was the Norse god of thunder. In some parts of the country, up until relatively recently, the derivations of Wednesday and Thursday were preserved in their pronunciation. For example, in Northumbria as late as 1900, Wednesday was known as Wodensday and Thursday was known as Thorsday.

Friday: Named after Frigg or Freya, the wife of Woden. She is the Norse equivalent of Venus, the Roman goddess of love and beauty, after whom the day is named in other European languages. *Vendredi* in French and *Venerdi* in Italian.

Saturday: Saturn's day. Saturn was the Roman god of agriculture and this day is the only one without a northern European origin. In Scandinavian languages Saturday is called *Lordag* or *Loverdag* (from *lauther* foam) meaning bath day, since it was customary for the Vikings to wash themselves at the end of the week. As bathing was not popular with Anglo-Saxons they adopted a name from elsewhere.

D-DAY The D stands for Day, and is used to refer to military operations that have not yet had a specific date set for them, or when secrecy is necessary. In such situations, an H is also designated for Hour (H-Hour). The most famous D-Day was 6 June 1944, the allied invasion of Normandy, but the notation had also been used in World War I.

DEADLINE Originally referred to a line seventeen feet from the inner enclosure of military prisons during the American civil war which, if crossed by prisoners, would result in death.

DEBACLE French *Débâcle* Unleash.
This was particularly used to describe the melting of ice on a river, leading to a flood. Hence in English usage, it refers to a flood or now, to any disaster.

DEBUT French *Débuter* To lead, to take the first turn such as in a game of billiards or bowls.
Nowadays it is more commonly associated with a new musician's first performance. A debutante is, or was, a young girl taking her first turn in adult social life.

DECEMBER *See Months of the Year.*

DECOY Dutch *Kooi* A cage.
Decoys were camouflaged basketware tunnels of diminishing

width into which ducks were driven by specially trained dogs. Nowadays a decoy can be used for any device or plan that distracts someone while another action such as entrapment is carried out.

DECREPIT Latin *De-* Down, and *Crepare* To break or creak.

DEFECATE Latin *Defaecare* To cleanse, to purify.
Not typically considered to be an act of cleanliness, defecation does nonetheless cleanse the body.

DEFENCE Middle English *Fens* A fence, from Old French *Defens* Protected.
A fenced city is one that is well defended.

DEFINE Old French *Definir* To end, to terminate, to limit.
To define something is to terminate any uncertainty.

DELIRIOUS Latin *De* From and *Lira* A furrow.
Delirious people do not travel in a straight line such as they would if they remained in a furrow. *See also Furlong.*

DELTA Greek. The fourth letter of the Greek alphabet the capital style of which is written as a triangle Δ.
This is also the shape of the land that is reclaimed when a river, slowing as it reaches its final destination, deposits sediment that has been carried along in its water. *See also Meander.*

DEMENTIA Latin *De* Away from and *Mens* The mind.
See also Alzheimer's.

DEMIJOHN French *Damejeanne* Lady Jane.
This large bottle with a short neck, often used in small-scale alcohol production, has nothing to do with a man named John,

but rather with the image of a stout French lady. But who she was has been forgotten.

DEMOCRACY Greek *Demos* The people and *Kratos* Strength and power.
A democracy is government by the people who exercise their power through the ballot box. *See also Aristocracy and Autocrat.*

DENIM The cloth now used to manufacture jeans was originally made in France and takes its name from the town of Nimes where it was sold as *Serge de Nimes*.

DEPLETION Late Latin *Depletionem* Blood letting.
Nowadays used rather broadly, the term once had a very specific meaning and referred only to the depletion of blood.

DERRICK Any crane or device for lifting something invariably has a rope hanging from it that resembles a gallows. Thomas Derrick was a hangman at the time of Queen Elizabeth I (reigned 1558–1603) and is reputed to have despatched 3000 people, most of them at Tyburn.

DEVIL Old English *Deofol* Evil spirit from Greek *Diabolos* An accuser, slanderer.

DEVIOUS Latin *Devius* Out of the way, as in deviant.
The word did not come to mean deceitful until the seventeenth century before which time it meant hidden away from the mainstream such as something lying beside the road rather than being on it.

DEVOUT Latin *Devotus* Devoted.
The devout are devoted to a cause.

DEXTERITY Latin *Dexter* Right, as opposed to left.
> A right-handed man who works skilfully with his right hand is said to be dexterous. It is therefore inappropriate to describe an equally skilled left-handed person as dextrous. *See also Ambidextrous, Awkward and Gawky*.

DIAMOND Middle Latin *Diamantem*, from Latin *Adamantem* Hardest metal.
> Diamond is the hardest known naturally occurring mineral.

DIET Greek *Diaita* A restricted way of life.
> Originally the word could refer to any restriction, not just to food. The other meaning of diet, a meeting of a governing assembly, has quite a different origin and is from Latin *Dieta* A day's Work. The most famous being The Diet held in the German town of Worms in 1521 when The Holy Roman Emperor, carrying out the wishes of the Pope, issued an edict requiring Martin Luther's arrest.

DIG Anglo-Saxon *Dician* To make a ditch.

DILAPIDATE Latin *Dis* Apart and *Lapis* A stone.
> Signifying the disintegration or decay of stone as in a ruined building. So it is improperly used when applied to the disintegration of anything other than stone.

DINGHY Hindi *Dingi* A little boat.

DINOSAUR Greek *Deinos* Awesome and *Saura* Reptile.
> The term was coined as *Dinosauria* by English palaeontologist Richard Owen in 1842. *See also Stegosaurus*.

DIPHTHERIA German *Diphthera* Leather.
> This infectious disease causes a leathery membrane to form inside the throat.

DIPLOMA Greek *Diploma* Folded double.

A diploma was originally the passport of a messenger that was folded in half for convenience of carriage.

DIPSOMANIA Greek *Dipsa* Thirst and *Mania* Madness.

A dipsomaniac is someone who has an uncontrollable, some might say mad, craving for alcohol.

DISASTER Greek *Dus* Unfavourable, bad and *Astron* Star.

Stars were thought to influence all human actions. The word disaster conveys the notion that calamities are caused by the unfavourable position of planets or stars.

DISCOUNT Latin *Dis* Away and *Compter* To count.

A discount may be said to be counting away from a price.

DISCOVER Latin *Dis* Away and *Couvrir* To cover.

Discoveries are made by taking away a covering to reveal something that was previously undiscovered.

DISPARAGE Latin *Dis* Away, *Par* Equal and French *Parage* Equality of birth.

To suggest that a person is some distance away from being equal is to disparage them.

DISTURB Latin *Dis* Completely and *Turbare* To throw into disorder.

DITTO Italian *Detto* As aforesaid, from *Dicere* To say.

DIVA Italian *Diva* Goddess.

Now applied mainly to opera singers, the word can describe any highly respected woman. The same origin as Divine. Water divining, the ability to locate a source of water below the ground using the branch of a hazel bush, remains such a mystery that it has a name which suggests divine intervention.

DIVEST Latin *de Vestio* To undress, hence to deprive of.
Divest is the opposite of invest.

DOCK Flemish *Dok* Cage.
That part of court reserved for the accused. At one time the prisoner would have been held in a cage while being tried.

DOCTOR Middle Latin *Doctor* Teacher, scholar.
It was only in the sixteenth century that the term started to be mostly used by the medical profession. But the old meaning is still retained and a Doctorate is usually non-medical.

DODO Portuguese *Doudo, doido* Fool.
The flightless dodos, endemic to Mauritius, were deemed to be foolish by Portuguese explorers because they approached humans without fear and were thus easily slaughtered. The species was extinct by 1700.

DOG DAYS Latin *Caniculares Dies.*
Named after the 'dog-star' Sirius (*Canicula*), the brightest star after the Sun, which rose just before the Sun between 3 July and 11 August and ushered in the hottest time of the year.

DOLCELATTE Italian *Dolce* Sweet and *Latte* Milk.
A soft, blue, cow's-milk cheese.

DOLLAR German *Thaler* Valley.
Bohemian silver coins were minted at Joachimsthal – St. Joachim's Valley – in what is now the Czech Republic. When production moved to other locations the coins lost their

association with St. Joachim and became known simply as thalers, or 'valleys'. Dutch settlers in the New World took with them their guilders (also derived from *thaler*) and so was born the mighty dollar albeit with a slight variation in its name. There are two theories as to the origin of the dollar sign. One is that it was taken from the Spanish coat of arms, which depicts two pillars bound by an S-shaped ribbon; the other maintains that it evolved from the way in which money bags were marked by banks, first with a U superimposed on top of an S and then in a more simplified form with an S struck through with two lines, i.e. the U without its curved base.

DOLPHIN Greek *Delphys* Womb.
Dolphins, which are mammals, are among a small group of marine creatures with wombs.

DOMINO Latin *Domino* Master.
The game using tiles with different numbers of spots was named by monks who cried '*Domino* I am the master' when they won, but its origins are thought to be related to the Chinese tile game of Mah Jong. *See also Tiddlywinks.*

DOOLALLY British soldiers in India who were affected by the heat and showed signs of madness were housed in a sanatorium at *Deolali* near Bombay (Mumbai), while they waited for transportation home. Doolally, a corruption of the town's name, became slang for madness.

DOOM Old English *Dom* Judgment, condemnation.
In its original sense, the word was very closely associated with religion, or the intervention of some higher outside authority.

DORMER WINDOW Latin *Dormire* To sleep.

A dormer window is one in a sloping roof that provides light to a dormitory or sleeping place.

DORMOUSE Latin *Dormire* To sleep and English Mouse.

The dormouse can hibernate for six months at a time surviving on fat deposits accumulated during their summer waking months. Lewis Carroll's dormouse at The Mad Hatter's Tea Party kept dropping off to sleep. *See also Treacle.*

DOWDY Scandinavian *Dawdie* A dirty, slovenly woman.

DOZEN Teutonic *Deux* Two and *Zen* Ten.

A simple explanation unlike eleven and twelve. *See Eleven and Twelve.*

DRACONIAN Draco was a very strict Greek legislator in the seventh century BC. Draconian laws are those that are unnecessarily strict and severe.

DRUG Low German *Droge-vate* Dry barrels or vats, vessels used to store drugs, which usually consisted of dried herbs.

DRUID Old Celtic *Dru* Tree, Oak, and *Wid* To know.

Druids were the teachers of Celtic society who had a vast knowledge of the natural world and worshipped oak trees.

DUFFEL Duffel is a town near Antwerp in Belgium where the thick cloth much used to make weatherproof hooded duffel coats was first woven.

DUM DUM Dum Dum is the town in India where the soft headed bullets that expand on impact, thus causing a greater wound, were first made. They are now banned by international convention.

DUNGAREE Hindi *Dongari* A region near Bombay where the calico overalls were first used. Being cheap to make, they were most frequently used by labourers and navvies. *See also Navvy.*

DYNAMITE Greek *Dynamis* Power.

EAGER French *Aigre* Rough, severe or harsh.
In the first scene of Hamlet Shakespeare says 'It is a nipping and eager air'. His meaning is cold and harsh. *See also Vinegar.*

EARN Teutonic *Ernte* Harvest.
To earn is to harvest the fruit of one's labours.

EARWIG Old English *Ear* An undeveloped flower bud as in an ear of corn and *Wic* A hiding place or dwelling.
The favoured hiding place of these insects was an *earwic*, that is a flower bud. The popular notion that this insect has a propensity to crawl into the human ear is entirely erroneous brought about by there being two quite unconnected meanings of the word ear.

EAST Germanic *Austra-* Toward the sun.
Hence Australia takes its name, being in the easternmost part of the world from the point of view of the European explorers who first visited it. *See also North, South and West.*

EASTER Old English *Eastre* The name of an Anglo-Saxon pagan goddess whose feast day was in the spring at around the same time as the modern day Christian festival.

ECHO Greek *Echo* A sound.

EDDY Norse *Yda* A whirlpool.

EDUCATE Latin *Educo* To lead forth.
>Properly used, the word educate means to bring out the latent faculties of the mind rather than to instruct by imparting knowledge.

ELBOW Old English *Ell* The length of the forearm and Latin *Ulna* The bone in the forearm.
>The length of the forearm, defined precisely as that of King Henry I (reigned 100–1135), was used as a unit of measure. (A successor of the cubit, 300 of which were the length of Noah's Ark.) A bow is something that bends as in archery and an elbow is the bow or bend of the ell or forearm.

ELECTRICITY Greek *Elektron* Amber.
>The first research into static electricity was conducted in 650 BC by the Greek philosopher Thales of Miletoo, who studied the electrical properties of amber.

ELEVEN and **TWELVE** Teutonic. Eleven derives from the German *Ainlif* One left, that is after counting to ten you have one left over. Similarly twelve comes from the Gothic *Twa-lif* two left. Our higher numbers such as thirteen and fourteen are from three ten and four ten etc. *See also Dozen and Numbers.*

EMANCIPATE Latin *Ex* Away from and *Mancipare* To transfer property.
>So rather than referring to the act of giving something, such as an emancipated slave being given his freedom or an emancipated woman being given the vote, the word actually refers to what was transferred away from them, ie the slavery and the lack of suffrage.

EMBRACE Latin *In* In and *Bracchia* Arms.

EMBRYO Greek *En* In and *Bryein* To swell.
>The embryo develops into a foetus inside the swelling uterus.

EMMET Old English *Aemette* Ant.
>The word *emmet* is used by the Cornish to describe the tourists that descend on their part of the country every summer. *See also Grockle.*

ENCYCLOPEDIA Greek *En* In, *Kyklos* Circle and *Paideia* Education.
>An encyclopedia provides an all round education. *See also Bicycle.*

END Old English *Ende* The opposite side.
>So to travel 'to the ends of the Earth' does not imply that the Earth is flat, but in fact requires it to be round.

ENDORSE Latin *In* In and *Dorsum* The back as in dorsal fin.
>The word originally meant anything carried on the back; elephants were said to be endorsed with heavy loads. Its meaning is now limited to signing the back of documents.

ENEMY Latin *E* From, indicating a negative and *Amicus* A friend.
>An encmy is therefore a negative friend.

ENERGY Greek *En* In and *Ergon* Work.

ENGLAND The Angles were a tribe from Angeln on the Baltic coast of present day Germany who migrated to the British Isles during the fifth and sixth centuries AD. The word has become slightly corrupted to Engle Land but the French still use the original spelling *Angleterre* Angle Land.

ENIGMA Latin *Aenigma* and Greek *Ainissesthai* To speak secretly or mysteriously.

An enigma is a riddle with a secret meaning and so perfectly described the coded messaging system devised by the Germans, but intercepted by the British, during the Second World War.

ENORMOUS Latin *Ex* Out of and *Norma* The rule, the norm.

This implies that something needn't be of great size in order for it to be accurately described as enormous, but merely unusual in some way.

ENTANGLE Anglo-Saxon *Tangle* A small bough or twig.

Twigs were smeared with birdlime to catch birds which, when caught, were said to be entangled. Hence the modern usage meaning an inability to disengage.

ENTHUSE Greek *En* In and *Theos* God.

Originally enthusiasm referred only to a passion for religious matters, but has since come to refer to any area of interest.

ENTRY Latin *Intrare* To go into.

ENUNCIATE Latin *E* From and *Nuntius* A messenger.

Someone bringing a message takes particular care to speak clearly.

ENVOY French *Envoyer* To send.

An envoy is someone sent elsewhere to perform a task.

EPHEMERA Greek *Epi* For and *Hemera* A day.

An ephemeral item is one that lasts for a brief period of time perhaps for only one day. There is a species of mayfly whose

Latin name is *Ephemera* on account of their lives lasting no longer than one day.

EPIDEMIC Greek *Epi* Among and *Demos* The people.
An epidemic is a disease that spreads among all the people.

EPISTLE Greek *Epi* On the occasion and *Stellein* To send.
Originally the word referred to the occasion on which a message was sent, as opposed to the message itself.

EQUATOR Latin *Æquator diei et noctis* Equaliser of day and night.
Originally this was an imaginary line in the sky marking the passage of the sun on days when the day and night were of equal length. It was later applied to the same place on the surface of the Earth.

EQUINOX Latin *Aequus* Equal and *Nox* Night.
The equinox is when the length of the day is the same as that of the night and takes place in the spring as daylight increases and in the autumn as it diminishes.

ERADICATE Latin *E* From and *Radix* A root.
To permanently remove as when a plant is dug up by its roots.

ERMINE The pure white fur of the stoat is so called from it having originally been brought from Armenia.

EROTIC Greek *Eros* The god of love, lust and intercourse.
The famous statue in Piccadilly Circus, London, is not of Eros at all but of The Angel of Christian Charity a far more appropriate subject to commemorate Lord Shaftesbury (1801 –1885) the Victorian reformer who did much to improve working conditions in Britain.

ERROR Latin *Erro* To wander.
> Error has come to mean to wander from accuracy, but previously it simply meant to wander. For example, Ben Jonson wrote of a voyage as 'an error by sea'.

ERUDITE Latin *E* From and *Rudis* Rude.
> An erudite person is one whose learned manner is without any vulgarity or rudeness.

ETHIOPIA Greek *Aithein* To burn and *Ops* Face.
> The Greeks referred to all inhabitants of sub-Saharan Africa as Ethiopians believing the colour of their skin was due to burning by the sun.

ETYMOLOGY Greek *Etumon* True sense and *Logia* A study of.
> You are reading a book of etymology that studies the true sense of words.

EUNUCH Greek *Eune* Bed and *Echein* To have charge of.
> Castrated men were put in charge of the beds within harems since they could be trusted not to perform sexual indiscretions. The word therefore refers to the occupation rather than to the person who had undergone the operation.

EVIL Old English *Yfel* Bad, wicked.

EXAGGERATE Latin *Agger* To heap or pile up.
> Nowadays it still means to pile it on but in terms of speech rather than physically. *Agger* also meant earthwork fortification, something else that had to be piled up.

EXCHEQUER Anglo-French *Escheker* Chessboard.
> The Norman kings of England did their accounting using

counters and a roll of chequered cloth. The letter x was added to the word due to the false assumption that it had a Latin root.

EXORBITANT Latin *Ex* From and *Orbita* An orbit or track.
Hence to be exorbitant is to be so far from the normal track as to be beyond all bounds of reasonableness.

EXOTIC Greek *Exo* From outside.
Exotic was used to describe any items that originated outside the country, not just those that were elaborate and ornate. But since imports were invariably such things as exotic silks and ornate ceramics the two meanings were easily interchangeable.

EXTERMINATE Latin *Ex* From and *Terminus* Boundary.
To exterminate meant to eliminate by banishing over the boundary into another country.

EXTRAVAGANT Latin *Ex* Outside of and *Vagare* Wander, roam (as in Vagrant).
To be extravagant is to be different or exotic. *See also Vagabond.*

FACSIMILE Latin *Facere* To make, to do and *Similis* Similar.
If you make a similar one you have created a facsimile.

FACTORY Latin *Facere* To make, to do.
The first factories were created in China in 750 BC.

FAMILY Latin *Famulus* A slave *Familia*, the collective noun,
referred to all the slaves of a household.

FAMINE Latin *Fames* Hunger.

FAN Latin *Vannus* A basket in which corn was tossed into the air to
winnow it in order to separate the wheat from the chaff.

FARCE Latin *Farcire* To stuff.
Miracle plays were often extended by the addition of light
hearted interludes of humour that were stuffed into the
traditional script. The derivation also explains how a Tomato
Farcie is one that is stuffed with something.

FAREWELL Anglo-Saxon *Fare* A passage.
We retain the original meaning in thoroughfare. Farewell
means 'may all be well on your passage'.

FARM Anglo-Saxon *Feorm* Supper, food or hospitality.

One of the conditions of land tenancy was that the tenant would supply their lords with specified quantities of food, known as *ferme*, from their tenanted land. The land on which this food was produced also became known as the *ferme* and this later became the farm. *See also Tithe.*

FARRIER Latin *Ferrum* Iron.

Farriers use iron to make horse shoes.

FASCISM Latin *Fascis* Bundle.

In ancient Rome, the symbol of power of the civic magistrates was the *fascis*, a bundle of white birch rods tied around an axe and carried by their Lictors, or bodyguards. The bundle of sticks represented strength through unity since one stick is easily broken whereas a bundle is not. Both the axe and the sticks could also be used to carry out sentences imposed by the magistrates. Italian dictator Benito Mussolini (1883–1945) adopted the symbol for his National Fascist Party as part of his attempt to emulate the earlier Roman Empire.

FEBRUARY *See Months of the Year.*

FELON Gaelic *Faell* To deceive or betray.

FENDER An abbreviation of de-fender. A piece of furniture that defends the house against sparks from the fire.

FERN Scandinavian *Fer* A feather.

The fronds of some ferns resemble feathers. The Greek word for fern is *Pterin*, which also means feather.

FERRET Latin *Fur* A thief.

The name seems to have originated because of the furtive or stealthy, thief-like habits of the ferret.

FIASCO Italian *Fiasco* A flask.

> If Venetian glass blowers created a flaw in their delicate work they turned the article into a flask, hence any failure became known as a fiasco.

FILLET Old French *Fil* Thread.

> The term was applied to cuts of meat on account of their being tied up with thread for storage.

FIRKIN Anglo-Saxon *Feowr* Four, *Kin* A diminutive.

> A firkin is a small cask holding a fourth part of a barrel equal to 9 gallons or 41 litres.

FLAMBOYANT French *Flamboyer* To flame.

> If something is flamboyant, it is spectacular and showy, like a fire. *See also Flamingo.*

FLAMINGO Provencal *Flamenc* Relating to a flame, specifically in reference to its colour. *See also Flamboyant.*

FLANNEL Welsh *Gwlanen* Wool.

> This became *flannen* before it became flannel.

FLATTERY Norman *Fladra* To pat or to stroke, as well as the wagging of a dog's tail.

> Many north European languages use the same word for flattery as they do for wagging a tail. If you flatter someone you heap praise on them, albeit falsely. Patting and stroking conveys the same message to a dog which will inevitably wag its tail as you do so.

FLIRT French *Fleureter* To talk sweet nothings.

FOB Old French *Forbe* Cheat.

To fob someone off is to tell them a lie in order to divert their attention thus they are cheated of the truth.

FOLIO Latin *Folium* A sheet of paper.

FONDUE French *Fondre* To melt.

Small pieces of meat and bread are dipped into melted cheese.

FOOL (As in dessert, such as gooseberry fool.) French *Foulé* Milled, mashed or pressed.

The derivation of this dessert has no association with stupidity.

FORNICATE Latin *Fornix* A brothel, where fornication, sexual intercourse between unmarried people, invariably takes place.

FORTNIGHT Old English *Feorwertyne* Fourteen and *Niht* Nights.

Few other languages have a word to describe a period of two weeks and it is little used in America.

FOSSIL Latin *Fossilis* Dug up.

FRANC French *Francorum Rex* The King of the Franks.

The French currency now replaced by the euro derived its name from this early inscription on the coins. The Franks were a German tribe who invaded Roman Gaul in AD 200–400.

FREELANCE The term now applied to a self-employed person available to work for any employer was originally given to a mercenary soldier in the Middle Ages who was free to be employed as a lancer in any army that needed his services.

FREEMASON French *Frère-maçon* Brother mason.

> With the corruption of the phrase came a corruption of its meaning and even the most high-ranking officials of the fraternity still erroneously refer to themselves as Free Masons rather than Brother Masons.

FRESCO Italian *Fresco* Fresh.

> Frescoes are paintings applied to fresh plaster that is still wet enabling the paint to sink into the surface.

FRIAR Latin *Frater* A brother.

FRIDAY *See Days of the Week.*

FRIEND Old English *Froend* To love.

FUEL French *Fowaille* A fireplace.

FÜHRER German *Führen* To lead.

> Hitler modelled his title on that chosen by Mussolini, Italian *Duce* Leader. *See also Nazism and Fascism.*

FUMBLE Norwegian *Falma* To grope.

FUNNEL Welsh *Ffynel* Air hole.

FUNNY-BONE The name given to that part of the elbow that produces an intense tingling when struck is a pun on the bone's Latin name *humerus* and consequently has nothing to do with humour at all. The tingling is actually caused by a blow to the ulnar nerve.

FURLONG Old English *Furh* Furrow and *Lang* Long.

> A furlong was the length of a furrow in one acre of land

when an acre was defined as having fixed dimensions of one chain (66 feet) wide by ten chains or one furlong long. This was considered to be the maximum area that an oxen could plough in one day. The long thin shape was important because it is difficult to turn a plough being pulled by oxen so they went in a straight line for a furlong before that was necessary. So an acre was one furrow long which became corrupted to a furlong. There are eight furlongs in a mile. *See also Acre, Delirious and Mile.*

FUSELAGE   French *Fuselé* Spindle-shaped.

The body of an aeroplane resembles the spindle around which newly spun wool was wound. The spindle is thought to be the oldest piece of technology known to man.

GAB Anglo-Saxon *Gabben* To prate, to talk excessively.
Hence the gift of the gab. The slang word 'gob' to refer to the mouth probably derives from the same root.

GALAXY Greek G*alaxias* Milky circle.
Our sun is a star at the centre of the solar system which is part of a galaxy known as The Milky Way containing in excess of 300 million stars. It is so called because the light from the millions of stars resembles a spilt glass of milk. Astronomers have estimated that there are more than 100 billion galaxies.

GALLOP Anglo-Saxon *Gehlopen* To leap or jump.

GAMMON Old French *Gambon* A leg.
Gammon is cured meat taken from the hind legs of a pig.

GARGLE Old French *Gargouiller* Throat.
A gargoyle is a carved, stone figure, usually grotesque in appearance, that projects from the side of a roof to convey rain water which flows through its throat and out of its mouth.

GAS Greek *Khaos* Atmosphere.
The word was coined by Jan Baptist van Helmont (*d.*1644)

a Flemish chemist and physician who was the first person to realise that the atmosphere was composed of different gases.

GASTRIC Greek *Gaster* Belly. Referring to the stomach.
Hence gastroenteritis is an inflammation of the intestine.

GAUZE French *Gaze*.
This material is believed to have originated from Gaza in Palestine.

GAWKY Middle English *Awk* Back-handed, left-handed.
Left-handed people were once thought to be clumsy because they were unable to use their right hands as effectively as right-handed people. Many tools such as scythes for cutting hay and corn were made specifically for right-handed people and left-handers using a scythe made specially for them would not be able to join a team of harvesters working their way across a field as they would be mowing in a different direction. *See also Ambidextrous, Awkward, Dexterity and Southpaw.*

GAZE Swedish *Gasa* To stare.
A gazebo is a summerhouse positioned so as to gaze at a splendid view.

GAZETTE Italian *Gazza* A magpie and *Gazetta* Idle chattering, reminiscent of the sound of magpies.
The word originated in Venice, where the newspapers or gazettes were full of chattering tittle-tattle. The word has also been attributed to the *gazatta*, a small coin supposedly used to buy the newspaper, however doubt may be cast on that attribution as the value of the Venetian *gazatta* never exceeded that of an English farthing, too small a sum to purchase a printed sheet.

GAZUMP Yiddish *Gezumph* To swindle.

Gazumping is the dishonest disregard of a spoken agreement before a contract can be signed. Gazundering is when a buyer lowers his verbal offer before signing a contract. Gaz(ump) and under.

GECKO Javanese *Gekok* The shrill cry of the lizard that has adhesive pads on its feet that enable it to run up walls.

GENE Greek *Genes* Born.

A gene is the basic unit of heredity that defines the character of a living organism as soon as it is born.

GENITAL Latin *Genitum* To beget.

GENOCIDE Greek *Genos* Race and Latin *Caedere* To kill.

The word was first used by Raphael Lemkin in 1933 to describe the Iraqi extermination of Assyrians and again after World War II when Nazi leaders were charged with the crime.

GENUFLECT Latin *Genu* The knee and *Flectere* To bend.

The act of bending the knee in prayer. *See also Knee.*

GEOGRAPHY Greek *Ge* Earth and *Graphein* To write.

A geography was originally a book that described the natural features of the earth and has, more recently, come to describe the study of such matters.

GEOLOGY Greek *Ge* Earth and *Logos* Speech.

Geology is therefore talking about the earth.

GEOMETRY Greek *Ge* Earth and *Metron* A measure.

Geometry is the division of mathematics relevant to the

measurement of shape, size and volume and was originally primarily concerned with the dimensions of the Earth and the universe.

GEORDIE Natives of Tyneside are called Geordies either because they supported the royalist cause of King George II in the Jacobite rebellion of 1745, or because the miners of that area preferred to use a safety lamp devised by George Stephenson rather than the better known one invented by Humphrey Davy.

GEOSTATIONARY Greek *Ge* Earth and *Statikos* To stand still.
A satellite in a geostationary orbit circles the earth at the same speed as the Earth's rotation and therefore appears to stand still, remaining above the same point on the earth's surface. To achieve this the satellite must be 22,000 miles above the Equator.

GERANIUM Greek *Geranos* A Crane.
The common name of the geranium is Cranesbill, named after the crane, a long-legged and long-necked wading bird, due to the resemblance of parts of the flower to the shape of the bird's head. *See also Pedigree.*

GERIATRIC Greek *Geras* Old age and *Iatros* Physician.
Geriatrics is the study by doctors of the conditions of old age.

GERRYMANDER American. Elbridge Gerry (1744–1814) Governor of Massachusetts manipulated the borders of constituencies in his state to favour his own party. The ruse was noticed when a map of the new boundaries was seen to resemble the shape of a salamander but a wag observed that it was instead a gerrymander. None the less he went on to become the fifth vice-president of the United States.

GEYSER Icelandic *Geysir* A famous erupting spring, from *Gjósa* To gush.

The first geyser to be known to Europeans is the Great Geyser in western Iceland which sends boiling water sixty metres into the air.

GHERKIN German *Gurcke* Cucumber and Anglo-Saxon *Kin* Small.

A gherkin is a small member of the cucumber family

GHETTO Italian *Ghetto* A foundry.

Jewish quarters of cities became known as ghettos after the main Jewish district of Venice, where there was an iron foundry.

GHILLIE Gaelic *Gille* A lad, servant.

A young man who assists a sportsman at hunting or fishing. Historically, he was a lad who attended a Highland chieftain.

GIBRALTAR Arabic *Gibel el Tariq ibn Ziyad* The mountain of Tariq ibn Ziyad.

Tariq was the leader of the Saracens when they invaded Spain in AD 711 and he fortified the rock as a base for his operations. *See also Morris Dancing and Tariff.*

GIN Dutch *Ginivra* and French *Genievere* Juniper.

The flavour of gin is obtained from the juniper berry. At one time gin was known as Geneva, not because it has any specific connection with the city of Geneva in Switzerland but because the place also derives its name from the plant.

GINGERLY Latin *Gentius* Well-born.

To act gingerly is to act cautiously, daintily, as though born of the gentry.

GINGHAM Malay *Ginggang* Striped.
> Gingham is a cloth woven in two colours arranged in stripes.

GIRL Middle English *Gyrle* A child of either sex.
> *See also Boy.*

GLADIATOR Latin *Gladiolus* A sword.
> The favoured weapon of the professional fighters who fought against each other and wild animals for the amusement of Romans. *See also Gladiola and Sedge.*

GLADIOLA Latin *Gladiolus* A sword.
> The plant has sword-shaped leaves. *See also Blade, Gladiator and Sedge.*

GLASS Celtic *Glâs* Green.
> The colour of glass when seen edgeways. Alternatively, the word may be derived from the Latin *Glacies* Ice.

GLIB Low German *Glibberig* Smooth, slippery.
> A person or speech described as glib is figuratively smooth or slick.

GLIDE Old English *Glidan* To slip.
> To slip suggests movement with a lack of control quite different from gliding that now tends to describe a more graceful and managed action.

GLOAT Norse *Glotta* To grin.
> Someone who displays a gloating expression of self-satisfaction invariably grins as he does so. *See also Grin.*

GLUCOSE Greek *Glykys* Sweet.
> Glucose is sugar that occurs naturally and was therefore the only sweetness that was available in ancient Greece.

GLUTTON Latin *Glutire* To devour.
   A glutton is someone who devours more food than is necessary.

GOB Old French *Gober* To gulp down.
   Goblet derives from the same root.

GONG Malay. Clearly onomatopoeic since it resembles the sound
   of the instrument, this word was first coined in Malaya where
   gongs play an important part in religious festivals.

GOOLIE Hindustani *Goli* A ball. Enough said!

GORSE Welsh *Gores* Waste land.
   Gorse, the highly invasive, prickly shrub that is a member of
   the pea family, is usually one of the first plants to become
   established on waste land.

GOSSIP Old English *Godsibb* Godparent, relative.
   The word was extended in Middle English to mean any close
   friend with whom one is likely to gossip.

GOULASH Hungarian *Gulyas* A herder of cattle.
   Goulash, a stew of beef, vegetables and spices, was the staple
   dish of the herdsmen on the plains of Central Europe.

GRADUAL Latin *Gradus* Step.
   A gradual progress may be said to be one step at a time.

GRAFFITI Greek *Graphein* To write.
   Writing is a somewhat grand description for some of the
   mindless daubs that adorn modern city walls.

GRAMMAR Greek *Grammatik* A letter of the alphabet.
   Grammar is the use of letters of the alphabet correctly and
   efficiently to create words and sentences.

GRANGE Anglo-Saxon *Grainage* A place where rent was paid in grain.

The word has come to describe a large country house such as the one where the landlord may have lived.

GRAVITY Latin *Gravis* Weight.

When Isaac Newton studied gravity and the movement of the planets he described the forces that defined their orbits as universal gravitation having established that it was a similar force that famously caused his apple to fall to the floor. *See also Aggravate.*

GREGARIOUS Latin *Gregis* A flock.

Animals or people that gather in a flock are said to be gregarious. *See also Congregate and Segregate.*

GRENADE French *Grenade* Pomegranate.

A grenade is an iron shell, filled with gunpowder and pieces of iron, that resemble the seeds of a pomegranate. Grenadiers were soldiers who, because of their height and therefore long arms, were able to throw grenades the furthest distance.

GRIMACE Anglo-Saxon *Grima* Mask.

Ancient comic masks were so distorted that hideous or distorted expressions of the human face were known as a *grima*, or grimace.

GRIN Old English *Grennian* Show the teeth, To Snarl.

To grin was originally a gesture of anger rather than mirth. *See also Gloat.*

GRIZZLY French *Gris* Grey.

Grizzly bears (Latin *Ursus horribilis*) take their name from their colour and not from the alternative meaning of the word – to grumble and whine.

GROCER French *Grosse* Unbroken packages.

Grocers were originally wholesalers, that is, people who deal in bulk or unbroken packages supplying retailers who break open the packs to sell in smaller quantities.

GROCKLE Used to describe non-Devonians by the people native to the county, *Grockle* was originally the name of a magical dragon in a Dandy comic strip called *Danny and his Grockle*. A Torquay man apparently applied it in the 1960s to a pensioner on holiday and the word was popularised by the 1962 film *The System* while it was being filmed in the town. *See also Emmet.*

GROG Admiral Edward Vernon (1684–1757) ordered in 1745 that men under his command should no longer be allowed to drink undiluted rum. Henceforth, his dissatisfied sailors contemptuously referred to the new diluted tipple as 'grog', after the Admiral's nickname Old Grog which in turn was derived from his custom of wearing a coat and breeches made of the coarse, stiffened fabric, grogram.

GROTTY An abbreviation of grotesque, meaning dirty or disgusting. It was first used by Beatle George Harrison, who, in the 1964 comedy *A Hard Day's Night*, described a range of shirts as being grotty, slang for grotesque.

GRUDGE Old French *Grouchier* To mumble, to grumble.

When a person holds a grudge against somebody, they are likely to grumble about him or her behind their backs.

GRUEL French *Gruau* Oatmeal.

Cereals such as oatmeal are boiled in either water or milk to make gruel.

GUILLOTINE Joseph Ignace Guillotin was a Parisian physician who, when elected to The National Assembly, proposed that decapitation should be used, not just for noblemen, but as the sole method of execution. However, he neither invented the machine nor, as is commonly asserted, did he perish by it. After a short period in prison during the reign of terror he founded the Academy of Medicine in Paris and died in 1814 aged 76.

GYMKHANA Hindi *Gend* Ball and *Khana* House.
A gymkhana was a venue for any sporting event – particularly those involving ball games. However the favourite sporting pursuits of Englishmen in India involved horses and they only used the word to describe equestrian events. When the word travelled back to Britain it was this meaning that came with it. In India and elsewhere in the Far East the term gymkhana still refers to a club where members take part in a variety of social and sporting activities both with and without horses.

GYMNASIUM Greek *Gymnos* Naked.
Greek athletes invariably competed without clothes.

GYNAECOLOGY Greek *Gynaikeios* Womanly and *Logia* Study.

HABEAS CORPUS Latin *Habeas Corpus* You should have
the body.

The Latin has been retained in English usage and refers
to the writ ordering that a jailer either gives freedom
to their prisoner or else produces them before a judge.
Considered a cornerstone of legal systems around the
world, the writ has nevertheless been suspended at various
times throughout history, in England during the World
Wars; during the Northern Irish troubles and more recently
in the United States where indefinite unlawful detention
has been legitimized as part of their War on Terror.

HALLUCINATE Latin *Hallucinari* Wander about in the mind.

To let your thoughts stray.

HAMMOCK Taino (Bahamas) *Hamacas* Sleeping net.

This type of bed, suspended between two trees, kept the
sleeper away from dampness and dirt, as well as snakes, spiders
and other harmful creatures on the ground. They were made
of bark from the *Hamacas* tree. They were known in ancient
Greece but the word hammock was introduced to Europe by
Christopher Columbus who brought a great many back from
his first voyage to what is now the Bahamas.

HANDKERCHIEF French *Couvre* Cover and *Chef* Head.

> In certain orthodox or devout religious groups a kerchief is a small piece of cloth for covering the heads of women. A handkerchief is similar but is held in the hand.

HARSH Scandinavian *Harske* Of a coarse texture.

> The meaning of the word has now broadened to refer equally to something of a coarse texture and also to something of a figuratively coarse nature.

HAVOC Celtic *Hafoc* Hawk.

> Havoc describes the devastation caused by a hawk if it lands in a poultry yard. To play havoc was also a military command to plunder captured territory.

HAZELNUT In most northern languages *hase* or similar means the husk, beard or shell of a fruit. Dutch *Hase*, Norwegian *Hasl*, Danish *Hase*. A hazel nut is therefore a bearded nut.

HEAD Anglo-Saxon *Heved* Heaved up.

> The head is raised above the rest of the body.

HEATHEN German *Heidin* Dweller upon heaths.

> When Christianity was introduced to Germany the wild dwellers on the heaths resisted conversion to the new religion. The term also applies to people who are not Muslim or Jewish. *See also Pagan.*

HEAVEN Anglo-Saxon *Haefen* Raised or elevated.

HEIRLOOM Latin *Heres* Beneficiary and Anglo-Saxon *Loma* Household items.

> In the days when all the family's clothes were spun and woven at home the loom was the most important article of

furniture in the house. Later the word was used to describe all household furniture that would be passed down from generation to generation.

HERMIT Greek *Eremites* Desert.
A hermit lives a life of seclusion in a deserted place.

HEROIN Coined as a trademark in the nineteenth century, the word heroin derived from *Hero* on account of the drug's effect, which was purported to bestow feelings of courage and strength upon those who took it. *See also Morphine.*

HERRING Anglo-Saxon *Hær* Army.
So numerous were the fish that an army best described their numbers.

HIBERNATE Latin *Hibernus* Wintry.
To hibernate is to pass the winter months in a dormant state.

HIMALAYA Sanskrit *Hima* Snow and *Alaya* Abode.

HINGE Old English *Hing* To hang.
A hinge is the hook on which a door is hung.

HIPPOPOTAMUS Greek *Hippos* Horse and *Potamos* A river.
Quite how this clumsy aquatic beast could have been named after a horse is not explained but possibly because they can run at 25mph (40kph), not a lot slower than a galloping horse. Their closest living relations are, surprisingly, whales and porpoises. *See also Walrus.*

HISTRIONIC Greek *Histrio* An actor.
Theatrical and melodramatic actions are most often performed by actors.

HOCKEY Old French *Hoquet* A shepherd's crook on account of the similarity in appearance of the hockey stick to the crook.

HOCUS POCUS Latin *Hoc est corpus* This is my body.
The expression that now refers to anything magical or miraculous is derived from words spoken by Christ that now form part of the communion service.

HOLIDAY A corruption of Holy day. At one time, religious festivals were the only times at which people did not work.

HOLLYHOCK Anglo-Saxon *Hoc* Mallow.
Hollyhocks are garden mallows indigenous to the Holy Land. Hence, holy or holly hock.

HOLOCAUST Greek *Holo* Whole and *Kaustus* Burnt.
A holocaust is an event when everything from people to property is burnt.

HONCHO Japanese *Han Cho* Squad leader.
The term, often now prefixed with 'head', refers to any leader.

HONEYMOON Romans considered honey to be the food of the gods and thus it featured prominently in their wedding ceremonies. The word 'honeymoon' is derived from the ancient practice of the bride and groom drinking mead for a period of one moon (one month) after their wedding. When a groom carries his bride over the threshold, he is perpetuating another Roman custom, that of keeping the bride's gown from the doorstep, which would have been smeared with honey as a blessing.

HOOCH Inupiaq (north and west Alaska) *Hoochino* The name of a tribe who made strong liquor from a distillation of fermented corn.

HOOLIGAN Derived from Houlihan's gang, an unruly Irish family.

HORDE Turkish *Ordu* A camp.
Hordes were nomadic tribes that seldom remained in permanent settlements, preferring to live in temporary camps instead.

HORIZON Greek *Horos* Limit.
A horizon marks the limit of your vision.

HORMONE Greek *Hormon* To stir up.
Hormones are bodily secretions transported to parts of the body where they stir up activity.

HOROSCOPE Greek *Hora* Hour and *Skopos* To observe.
A horoscope makes observations based upon the precise hour at which a person was born.

HORSERADISH The word horse was often used synonymously with large or powerful. Hence the meaning has remained in particular reference to the horseradish, which has a very strong flavour. Radish is from Latin *Radix* A Root.

HUMBLE Latin *Humus* The ground.
A humble person is someone who lives a lowly, unpretentious existence, so low in fact that they might appear close to the ground.

HUMBLE PIE Saxon *Umble* The entrails of a deer.
The best cuts of the venison were reserved for the lord of

the manor whereas those who sat below the salt, i.e. the Saxons following the Norman conquest, had to make do with the inferior portions, or umble. Hence, those whose pie was made with umble were accepting their humiliation as one does when humbly making an apology – a situation now termed 'eating humble pie'. The connection between umble and humble is therefore rather more than just a pun, since it was the humble people who ate the umble pie. *See also Animals and Venison.*

HUSBAND Anglo-Saxon *Hus* A house and *Bonda* Master.

HYDRAULIC Greek *Hydor* Water and *Aulos* A pipe.

HYPOTENUSE Greek *Hypoteinousa* Stretching under.
The hypotenuse is the line opposite the right angle of a right-angled triangle, thus looking as though it has been stretched between the ends of the two shorter sides.

HYSTERIA Greek *Hystera* The uterus.
The Greeks believed that only women suffered from hysteria. This was due to an assertion made by Hippocrates, often considered to be the father of medicine, that it was caused by the uterus rising up in the body and compressing the heart, lungs and diaphragm.

ICEBERG German *Eis* Ice and *Berg* A hill.

IDEAL Latin *Idealis* Existing in idea.
Idealistic notions often have no basis in reality.

IDIOT Greek *Idiotes* A private citizen, as opposed to a public official.
The English word idiot originally had the same meaning,
but in time it came to refer only to rude or ignorant rustics.
Today it tends to describe someone who is born without
understanding, a natural fool, as opposed to someone who
chooses to behave stupidly.

IGLOO Inuit *Iglu* House.
Igloos were rarely used as permanent dwellings but were
constructed by hunters needing a temporary shelter when
away from home. *See also Teepee.*

ILLUSION Latin *Illudere* To mock.
Illusions were once the preserve of conjurors who mocked
their audiences with tricks and hoaxes.

IMPALE Latin *In* In and *Palus* A stake.
Vlad the Impaler, *d.*1476 (otherwise known as Dracula and

the inspiration for Bram Stoker's novel) was a sadistic torturer who impaled his enemies on stakes and is reputed to have murdered up to 100,000 people in this way.

IMPEACH Latin *Impedicare* To fetter.
A leader who is impeached is prevented from continuing in office as effectively as fetters or leg irons would prevent them from walking.

IMPLORE Latin *In* In and *Plorare* To weep.
A person imploring is making a request so earnestly that they may be reduced to tears.

INCARCERATE Latin *In* In and *Carcer* A prison.

INCH Latin *Uncia* A twelfth part.
An inch is a twelfth part of a foot.

INCOGNITO Latin *In* Not and *Cognitus* Known.
The term was originally applied only to sovereigns or princes who assumed fictitious names and dispensed with their retinues when they did not wish to be recognised.

INERT Latin *Inertis* Idle, lazy.
Alert is wide-awake, active and lively, inert on the other hand is sleepy, sluggish and indolent.

INFANT Latin *Infans* Speechless.
An infant is a child who has not yet learned to speak.

INFANTRY Latin *Infante* Youth.
The infantry were originally the youngest soldiers and those of low rank who did not merit inclusion in the smarter cavalry regiments.

INGENIOUS Latin *Ingenium* Mother-wit.

Ingenuity was considered to be a natural ability, that is, an ability present in some at birth and therefore mother given.

INGOT Anglo-Saxon *In* In and *Geotan* To pour.

Ingots are made by pouring liquid metal into moulds.

INN Old English *Inne* Student lodging.

The Inns of Court, the associations of which barristers must be accredited also provided accommodation for their members.

INOCULATE Latin *In* In and *Oculus* An eye or more relevant here a bud.

The original meaning was the insertion by grafting of a bud into the stem of another plant by a gardener so that it would grow there. Medical inoculation is the insertion of a mild strain of a disease so that it will grow sufficiently to induce immunity. *See also Vaccine.*

INSECT Latin *In* In and *Seco* To cut as in secateurs.

An insect is a creature that has an apparent separation, or cut, between the head and the thorax.

INSULAR Latin *Insula* Island.

If something is insular, it is like an island in that it is isolated or separate.

INSULIN Latin *Insula* Islet.

The hormone that regulates glucose in the blood is produced in a part of the pancreas called the Islets of Langerhans.

INSULT Latin *In* In and *Salto* To leap.

Originally it meant to leap onto the land of an enemy. What could be more insulting than to find that someone had leapt onto your land?

INTERLOPER Dutch *Interlooper* A smuggler and *Loopen* To enter running.
Captured smugglers were made to run into court between two customs officers.

INTERNET From *Inter*national and *Net*work.

INTESTINE Latin *Intus* Inside.

INTREPID Latin *Intrepidus* Without trembling.
An intrepid person is one who shows no sign of fear and therefore does not tremble.

INUIT Inuit *Inuit* People.
The Eskimos of northern Canada and Greenland call themselves Inuits, which in their language means people, the plural of *Inuk* Person.

INVENTION Latin *Inventionem* A finding or discovery.
To invent something, therefore, means to find something that already exists rather than create something new.

INVINCIBLE Latin *Invincibilis*, from *In* Not, and *Vincibilis* Conquerable.

INVOICE Middle French *Invoyer* To send.
An invoice is a document sent to request payment. An envoy, from the same source, is someone who is sent to perform a task.

IODINE Greek *Iodes* Violet-like.
Iodine was first discovered by a salt-petre maker in Paris in 1812.

IRRIGATE Latin *In* Upon and *Rigare* To wet.

ISOBAR Greek *Isos* Equal and *Baros* Weight.
> An isobar is a line on a map joining places of equal pressure. The pressure is caused by the weight of the air above.

ISOTHERM Greek *Isos* Equal and *Therme* Heat.
> An isotherm is a line on a map joining places of equal temperature.

ISTHMUS Greek *Isthmos* A neck.
> An isthmus, such as the famous one at Corinth by which the Peloponnese are joined to the Greek mainland, has the appearance of a neck.

IVORY ·Sanskrit *Ibha* An elephant.
> Ivory was also obtained from the tusks of the walrus and narwhal.

IVY Gaelic *Eid* The plant that clothes.
> Ivy covers trees as if clothing them but rather than providing warmth and protection it will eventually kill the host. The word ivy has also come to us via other languages, such as Welsh *Eiddew* and Anglo-Saxon *Ifig*.

JACKASS Arabic *Jackhsh* One who extends his ears.

JACK RUSSELL This small terrier took its name from a Westcountry parson, the Revd Jack Russell, 1795–1883, who started the breed with Trump, a female he bought from a milkman for the purpose of ferret-hunting.

JANITOR Latin *Janua* A door.
> Janitors are now caretakers but originally they were doormen. From the same root as January, the door of the year. *See also Months of the Year.*

JANUARY *See Months of the Year.*

JAUNDICE French *Jaune* Yellow.
> The skin of jaundice sufferers becomes yellow due to an excess of bile.

JAVELIN Spanish *Jabalína* A wild boar. A boar-hunting spear.

JELLY Latin *Gelo* To congeal.

JERUSALEM Hebrew *Yaráh* A foundation and *Shalom* Peace.

Jerusalem is therefore translated into English as 'foundation of peace'.

JERUSALEM ARTICHOKE Italian *Girasole* Sunflower and *Articiocco* Artichoke.

The name is derived from the fact that the plant's flowers and leaves resemble those of the *Girasole* sunflower. The English term is therefore an absurd corruption of the Italian and has nothing whatsoever to do with Jerusalem. *Girasole* is derived from Italian *Gira* It turns to and *Sole* The sun, because every morning the flower heads face the sunrise and, during the day, they turn to follow the path of the sun across the sky. At night they turn back to await the next dawn. *See also Artichoke.*

JOB Old English *Gobbe* A lump.

The word job refers to a piece, or lump, of work needing to be done.

JODHPUR The tight fitting riding breeches originated in the city of Jodhpur in Rajasthan, India.

JOURNEYMAN French *Journée* A day's work.

The word does not refer to a journey, it describes someone who works for a daily wage.

JOVIAL Latin *Jove* Jupiter.

The Romans thought that each person was born under the particular influence of one of the planets. Hence a *jovial* person, one who was born under Jupiter, the planet of happiness, was joyful. Likewise, *martial* people were influenced by Mars, *mercurial* people by Mercury.

JUDGE Latin *Jus* Law and *Dicere* To declare.

JUDO Japanese *Jiu* Gentleness and *Do* Way.

Judo is a competitive sport that enables martial arts to be performed without injury.

JUGGERNAUT Sanskrit *Jagannatha* Lord of the universe, a name for the Hindu god Krishna.

Each year at the Jagannath Temple in Orissa, India, Krishna devotees hold a procession of chariots containing statues, among them an enormous effigy of Jagganath. So large is it that it has been known to slide out of control, crushing or injuring people in the crowd. British Christian missionaries in the colonial era spread the lie that Hindus were dangerous fanatics who threw themselves in front of the chariots in acts of misguided self-sacrifice. Henceforth, the word in English became synonymous with large unstoppable, destructive forces.

JUKE Bambara (A west African language) and Gullah (a Creole language that was developed in the southern United States by combining words from many languages brought over the Atlantic by slaves and English) *Juke* Bawdy. In America the term can refer to a juke box, as well as a juke house otherwise known as a brothel.

JULY *See Months of the Year.*

JUMBO Swahili *Jumbe* Chief.

Now applied not so much to some person or thing of importance but to anything of a great size, such as a jumbo jet. Use of the word to describe anything with an unusually large bulk derives from it being the name of a particularly large African elephant on display at London Zoo in 1865. Jumbo was bought by P. T. Barnum's circus and shipped to America in 1882 where he was accidentally hit and killed by a railway train in 1885.

JUNE *See Months of the Year.*

JUNGLE Sanskrit *Jangala* Uncultivated wilderness.

JURY Latin *Jurare* To swear.
> Members of a jury are asked to swear that they will reach a just and impartial verdict.

JUTE Sanskrit *Juta* Matted hair.
> In fact jute is a vegetable fibre, not hair, but presumably the material, also known as hessian and used for making sacks, takes its names from its resemblance to hair.

KAGOOL French *Cagoule* A monk's hood, or cowl.
   The lightweight waterproof coats have hoods that are similar to those of monks.

KALE Middle English *Cawul* Cabbage.
   Evidently in the Middle Ages a cabbage was a cabbage, and there was little, if any, differentiation made between different types. Coleslaw came to English from Dutch and is derived from *Kool* Cabbage, of similar derivation to *Cawul*, and *Sla* Salad.

KALEIDOSCOPE Greek *Kalos* Beautiful, *Eidos* Form and *Skopeein* To look.
   A kaleidoscope consists of a tube containing mirrors set at fixed angles so that they reflect numerous images of coloured beads which create a beautiful form to look at.

KAMIKAZE Japanese *Kami* Divine and *Kaze* Wind.
   During the Second World War kamikaze pilots were those who flew suicide missions, nose-diving their planes into Allied ships. They would be dispatched from their base with the farewell cry *'Kamikaze!'*, which is very similar in meaning to our God speed.

KANGAROO Guugu Yimithirr (Queensland, Australia) *Gangurru*
The Grey kangaroo.

This little known language is spoken by a few Aborigines in Queensland but it does seem to be the source of the word kangaroo, albeit with a slight variation due to a mishearing by an early explorer. Sadly this dispels the myth that kangaroo is Aborigine for 'I don't understand you', which was the reply given to Captain Cook when he asked a non English-speaking native the name of the animal.

KARAOKE Japanese *Kara* Empty and *Okesutora* Orchestra.
Karaoke is a form of entertainment for which words are removed from recordings of songs, leaving just the orchestra on its own.

KARATE Japanese *Kara* Empty and *Te* Hand.
The martial art teaches weaponless self-defence.

KEDGEREE Hindi *Kitchri*
A dish of smoked haddock, rice and eggs. The recipe was taken to India by Scottish soldiers serving there in the nineteenth century, where the dish was adapted and returned to the British Isles with a Hindi name.

KERFUFFLE Gaelic *Car* To turn and *Fuffle* To disarrange.
A kerfuffle is a state of confusion brought about by a lack of arrangement.

KETCHUP Malay *Kechap*, Chinese *Ketsiap*, Japanese *Kitjap*
Any type of sauce, not necessarily tomato.

KHAKI Persian *Khak* Dust, ashes.
Until the end of the nineteenth century British soldiers wore red uniforms and were universally known as redcoats. But

the development of snipers' rifles meant that a bright red garment was an easier target than one that blended in with the surroundings and the khaki battle dress was adopted before the Boer War. Many regiments retain red uniforms for ceremonial occasions.

KIBBUTZ   Hebrew *Qibbus* Gathering of people.
A kibbutz is an agriculturally-based, socialist commune, consisting of a gathering of like-minded people.

KIDNAP   Gypsy slang *Kid* A child and *Nab* To steal.
The word was originally *kidnabber* and so means to steal a child rather than an adult. We still use the word nab as in 'He nabbed my sweets'.

KIOSK   Turkish *Kosk*, from Persian *Kushk* Summer House.
Most European languages have a similar word for small detached structures that give shade to street vendors, but in Turkey the word also refers to a garden shelter such as a gazebo.

KIP   Danish *Kippe* Lodging or ale house.
Going for a kip meant looking for a lodging when you needed somewhere to sleep.

KNEE   Anglo-Saxon *Nicken* To bend.
Knuckles are from the same root. *See also Genuflect.*

KNIT   Old English *Cnyttaan* A knot.

KNOT   Latin *Nodus* A Knot. As in a measure of speed.
One knot is defined as being one nautical mile per hour. The speed of a ship is measured in knots and this was achieved using a rope knotted every 51 feet so that 120 measured a

nautical mile there being 6120 feet in a nautical mile. At one end was fixed a large flat piece of wood or a log. A floating log meets little resistance in the water and therefore remains stationery, so when thrown overboard from a moving boat the rope tied to it passes freely over the stern at the same speed that the ship moves forward. The 120 knots in the rope represents the number of half minutes in an hour so it follows that the number of knots that pass over the stern in half a minute represents the number of nautical miles travelled in one hour. *See also Mile.*

KOSHER Hebrew *Kasher* Right in the sense of being correct or as it should be.
This word refers to the procedures laid down in the Torah for the right way to prepare food.

KOWTOW Mandarin *K'o* Touch and *T'o* Head.
Subjects coming before the Chinese Emperor had to kneel and bow so low that their heads touched the ground.

KRAFT German *Kraft* Strength.
Kraft wrapping paper is strengthened to help it withstand damage in transit.

LABORATORY Latin *Labore* To work.

A laboratory is therefore any place of work not necessarily only those associated with scientific endeavours.

LACE Latin *Laqueus* A noose.

This derivation is relevant to all three of the word's primary meanings, a shoe lace, the delicate stitched fabric and the verb, each of which involve threading. Curiously, though, our word 'noose' derives from Latin *Nodus* Knot.

LACONIC The Spartans were parsimonious with words. On one occasion they were approached by a herald from the Athenian army who told the Spartan commander: 'If we come to your city, we will raze it to the ground.' The Spartan answer was the one word 'If'. From the name of the land of which Sparta was capital, Laconia, comes *laconic* meaning using few words. The leaders of Sparta imposed a strict militaristic lifestyle on the inhabitants, discouraging all forms of culture and from this we have the word Spartan meaning an austere existence.

LACROSSE French *Crosse* A bishop's crook.

The crook bears a resemblance to the stick used by lacrosse players. The sport of lacrosse, short for *le jeu de la crosse*, or 'the game of the Bishop's crook' was adapted from an ancient Native American practice known as *baggataway*. Unlike the modern version, it involved hundreds of players and a pitch up to one square mile in size. Its role in Native American culture was to train young men to be warriors, to settle inter-tribal disputes and, religiously, as entertainment for the Creator. When in 1763 French colonialists, impressed with the game but appalled by its violent nature, attempted to organize it by establishing a set of rules and reducing the number of players, the natives did not approve and massacred every one of them with their tomahawks.

LAGER German *Lager* Storehouse.
Lager beer is stored for a minimum of three weeks before it is served.

LARD Greek *Larinos* Fat and *Laros* Pleasant to taste.

LARVA Latin *Larva* Masked.
An insect in the grub stage of its life remains hidden or masked.

LASER An acronym standing for *L*ight *A*mplification by *S*timulated *E*mission of *R*adiation.

LAVATORY Latin *Lavare* To wash.
The *Lavitorium* was originally a vessel for washing in, later it become a room in which the vessels were kept. Since these washrooms invariably had lavatories as well they adopted the same name.

LAVENDER Latin *Lavare* To wash.
Romans placed the dried flowers of the Lavender plant in their wash tubs to add a pleasant aroma to their clean laundry.

LAW Old English *Lagu* Something laid down or fixed.

> The law is laid down by the government and enforced by their police.

LEGUME Latin *Legere* To gather.

> Once fully grown, the plants are gathered together for use. The word has the same root as Legion, which refers to a group of soldiers that have been gathered together to form a unit.

LEMUR Latin *Lemure* Ghost.

> Lemurs are long-tailed animals that live wild only in the Madagascar. They are grey, mainly nocturnal and have large staring eyes that give them a ghost-like appearance.

LENIENT Latin *Lenis* Soft.

> To be lenient is to be mild, tolerant or soft.

LENT Anglo-Saxon *Lenet* Length.

> The Anglo-Saxon name for March was *lenet-monat*, or length-month, due to the lengthening days. Lent, which falls mainly in March, is therefore a contraction of the Anglo-Saxon word for length.

LEOPARD Latin *Leo* Lion and *Pard* Panther.

> The leopard was anciently thought to be a cross between a lioness and a male panther. Its name was therefore a combination of the two.

LESBIANISM The earliest written references to same-sex love between women are in poems written by Sappho. She lived on the Greek Island of Lesbos in 600 BC.

LETTUCE Latin *Lactuca* Milk.

> The lettuce plant, introduced to England from the Netherlands

in 1520, is so named because of the milky sap that exudes from the stem when it is cut.

LEVANT Italian *Levant* Rising.
The eastern end of the Mediterranean is where the sun was seen rising.

LIBRARY Latin *Liber* The thin coating found on the inner bark of the Egyptian papyrus plant. This was the material used by the ancient Greeks and Romans for making paper, the word for which was also derived from *papyrus*. *See also Paper*.

LIEBFRAUMILCH German *Liebfrau* The Virgin Mary and *Milch* Milk.
This Rhineland wine was first made in a convent dedicated to The Virgin Mary.

LIMOUSINE Shepherds in the Limousin region of southern France wore distinctive hooded cloaks, a style of clothing that was popular with chauffeurs in the early days of motoring, that is, when the driver sat outside while the passengers had a separate enclosed compartment behind. The cloaks, which became known as Limousins, gave their name to the type of motor car they were used in. *See also Chauffeur*.

LINOLEUM Latin *Linum* Flax and *Oleum* Oil.
The floor covering was invented in 1869 by an Englishman who devised the name from the materials he used.

LITTER Anglo-French *Litere* A portable bed.
In order to make a comfortable bed, travellers would scatter straw or some other soft material. Over time, the term came to describe the scattered material alone and lost all association with bedding.

LOO French *Garde de l'eau* Watch out for the water.

In medieval times chamber pots were emptied from upstairs windows, often to the misfortune of unsuspecting pedestrians in the street below. This cry, often abbreviated to '*L'eau!*', was the only warning of what was about to befall them.

LOOT Hindi *Lut* A stolen thing.

LOVE Latin *Lubere* To please. Enough said!

LUKEWARM Celtic *Liegh* Half, partly.

Hence lukewarm is half warm.

LULLABY Middle English *Lullen* To lull, and *By*, as in good-bye.

Children are sung lullabies in order to lull them to sleep.

LYRICS Greek *Lyrikos* A lyre.

The ancient stringed instrument, originally using a tortoise shell as a sound box, was the precursor of the harp and generally provided the musical accompaniment when the lyrics of a song were being sung.

MACARONI Latin *Macarare* To crush.
During production the wheat is crushed to make flour for the dough. Macerate is from the same origin.

MACHINE Latin *Machina* and Greek *Makhos*. A contrivance.

MACKEREL Old English *Mackled* Spotted or speckled.
The fish has a speckled colouring.

MAD Old English *Gemaedde* To be out of one's mind. Insane is from the Latin *Sane* Healthy of which the negative is formed by the addition of the prefix *In*.
Insane originally meant to be unhealthy in body as well as in mind but the former was gradually dropped.

MADONNA Latin *Mea Domina* My lady.

MAGAZINE Middle French *Magasin* A storehouse, especially of military munitions.
Magazines, being storehouses of information rather than weapons, were first published in the eighteenth century.

MAGENTA Magenta, a fuchsia-red colour, is one of the three primary colours, the others being yellow and cyan, an aquamarine shade of blue. A perfect shade of magenta dye was developed in 1859, the same year as the battle of Magenta near Milan when a French and Sardinian army commanded by Napoleon III defeated an Austrian army.

MAGIC Avestan (An extinct language of the Zoroastrians of ancient Persia) *Magi* Sorcerer via Greek *Magike* Magus.
The Magi were astrologers and followers of the prophet Zoroaster who lived in present day Iran in approximately 600 BC. This would tie in with the origins of the three wise men visiting Jesus shortly after his birth but in no way explains how they came from the east after seeing a star in the east as that would have been behind them.

MAGNET The word magnet is derived from the city of Magnesia on the eastern coast of the Greek mainland where the magnetic quality of lodestone is said to have first been noticed.

MALARIA Latin *Malus* Bad and *Aeris* Air.
It was believed that malaria was caused by unhealthy air rising from swamps and marshes. In fact it is caused by a parasite in the blood of the *Anopheles mosquito* that thrives in undrained land.

MALLEABLE Latin *Malleus* A hammer.
A malleable material such as copper can be beaten or hammered into a different shape without breaking.

MAMMOTH Yakut (the language of the Sakha Republic, eastern Siberia) *Mama* Earth and Old Vogul (the language of the Mansi, western Siberia) *Memont* Earth-horn.
The great prehistoric elephant with 10 foot (3 metre) long tusks (or horns as the Mansi people called them), that became

extinct 10,000 years ago and now lends its name to anything of great size, is thought to have burrowed in the earth. This belief undoubtedly came about since the only evidence of these animals having existed was the occasional discovery of fossilized remains under the ground.

MANGER Latin *Manducare*, via French *Manger* To eat or to chew.
A manger is a trough to hold animal food such as the one that the baby Jesus was laid in when there was no room at the inn.

MANIFESTO Latin *Manifestare* To make public.
A manifesto makes public the policies of a political party seeking support prior to an election.

MANTELPIECE Latin *Mantellum* A cloak.
The mantel or mantle of a fireplace is the shelf from which wet coats or mantels were hung to be dried. In terms of a covering the word mantel is also used for a gas mantel that covers the flame and the Earth's mantel that covers the inner core.

MAP Latin *Mappa* A napkin.
The first maps were drawn onto sheets of cloth such as were used for napkins. *See also Napkin.*

MARATHON A marathon is a race of 26 miles 385 yards (42.195 kilometers). It commemorates the legend of Pheidippides, a Greek who ran from Marathon to Athens in 490 BC with news that the Greeks had defeated the Persian navy. He is reputed to have cried: 'We have won', before dropping dead. However, the precise length of the run is not the same that Pheidippides ran but the distance between Windsor Castle and The White City stadium which was the route of the race in the 1908 Olympic Games held in London.

MARBLE Latin *Marmor* Sparkling.

The Latin later came to describe gleaming or shiny stone and marble in particular.

MARCH *See Months of the Year.*

MARCH HARE The phrase 'as mad as a March hare' should actually be 'as mad as a *marsh* hare', since hares in wetland areas tend to rush about more as there is an absence of cover in marshland.

MARMALADE Portuguese *Marmelo* Quince.

A popular derivation for this word holds that Mary Queen of Scots, who spent much of her life in France, ordered orange jam whenever she was ill. The words '*Marie est malade*', or 'Mary is ill', are therefore supposed to have become synonymous with the preserve, the phrase being corrupted to 'marmalade'. However, since marmalade was originally made from the quince berry, Portuguese *Marmelo*, it is very likely that the word has a Portuguese derivation.

MARSH Gaelic *Mar* A pool.

MATRIX Latin *Matrix* A womb, from *Mater* Mother (as in Maternal).

The sense of a matrix containing something has been retained and the word now more commonly refers to mathematical data tables, or in geology to a mass of rock containing gems and fossils.

MATTRESS Arabic *Al Matrah* A mattress. A place where anything is thrown.

Mattresses were thrown on the floor to provide sleeping quarters for travellers who carried their bedding with them.

MAUSOLEUM Derived from the tomb of Mausolus, King of
Caria, erected in AD 353 in present day Turkey. It was destroyed
by an earthquake and its stones were then used by crusaders
to build Bodrum Castle. It was one of the Seven Wonders of
the Ancient World, the others being The Hanging Gardens of
Babylon, The Temple of Artemis at Ephesus, The Colossus of
Rhodes, The Statue of Zeus at Olympia, The Lighthouse of
Alexandria and the Great Pyramid of Giza. The latter being
the only one that remains.

MAY *See Months of the Year.*

MAYONNAISE Mahon, after which the sauce of egg yolks,
vinegar and oil is named, is the capital of Minorca in the
Balearic Islands. Mayonnaise's popularity in Britain dates from
the British occupation of Minorca between 1707 and 1713.

MEANDER The River Meander in Phyrgia, in modern-day Turkey,
wanders in a serpentine manner.

MEASLES French *Meseau* Leprosy.
Chaucer used this word to describe leprosy but since then
it has been applied to measles, the highly contagious disease
caused by a virus. German measles, a quite unrelated disease,
acquired its name from the same inaccurate source and was
first identified by German physicians. Its proper name *Rubella*
is derived from the Latin for Little Red a reference to the
colour of the rash that covers much of the body.

MEDIEVAL Latin *Medius* Middle and *Aevum* Age.
Medieval therefore means Middle Ages and is generally used
to describe the 1000 years between the fall of the western
Roman Empire and the Renaissance.

MEDITERRANEAN Latin *Medius* Middle and *Terra* Land.

The name of the sea dates from the time when it was the centre of the known world. The Romans called it *Mare Nostrum* Our Sea.

MELANCHOLY Greek *Melas* Black and *Chole* Bile.

Hippocrates believed that the body was filled with four substances: black bile, yellow bile, phlegm and blood, also known as the four cardinal humours, *melancholic, choleric, phlegmatic* and *sanguine*, the balance and interplay of which was supposed to dictate a person's temperament. Prolonged chronic depression was thought to be caused by an excess of black bile, hence the condition is known as melancholia.

MELODRAMA Greek *Melos* A song and *Drama* Action.

A melodrama was therefore a musical performance rather than an expression of overdramatic behaviour.

MENOPAUSE Greek *Men* Month and *Pausis* Cessation.

The cessation of a monthly event.

MEWS French *Muer* To change.

Mews are small streets behind grand town houses with stabling for horses and cages for hunting falcons. The birds were kept there while they were moulting and unable to hunt. Moulting is a natural process when birds change their feathers.

MICROBE Greek *Mikros* Little and *Bios* Life.

Microbes are very small living organisms. The word was coined in the nineteenth century when scientific research first became aware of them.

MICROFICHE Greek *Mikros* Little and French *Fiche* A small piece of paper or card such as a page.

The word was coined when the miniaturisation of pages, usually to about one twenty-fifth the size of the original, was devised in the twentieth century for storage purposes. This is usually a photographic process but the word can also apply to a printed page composed of miniature type.

MILE Latin *Mille* A thousand.

The Roman mile was equal to one thousand paces of a soldier with a pace being two steps. Each pace was 5 Roman feet, which was equivalent to 58 Roman inches. The Roman mile was 1618 modern yards in length and the modern English mile is 8 furlongs or 1760 yards. A nautical mile is defined by the Admiralty as 6080 feet (1853 metres), 15% more than a land mile, this distance being one minute of latitude in the south of England. A minute is 1/60th of a degree, there being 360 degrees in a circle, or around the world. A nautical mile is therefore 1/21600th of a line drawn around the world through London. *See also Furlong and Knot.*

MILLENNIUM Latin *Mille* One thousand and *Annus* A Year.

AD 2000, or AD 2001, if you are a perfectionist, was described as 'The Millennium', however the term is more accurately applied to a whole period of one thousand years and not simply the dawn of a new one.

MILLINER A Milaner is a native of Milan where the fancy goods market has always thrived. In particular they produced fashionable women's hats.

MINIATURE Latin *Minium* Red lead.

The word miniature, when applied to small paintings, has nothing to do with their size. It is derived from the practice of ornamenting the margins of books with pictures highly coloured with *minium*.

MINISTER Latin *Minister* Servant.

    Whether in the church or government, ministers are appointed to serve the community.

MINUTE A minute (as in time) is a minute (as in small) portion of an hour. So the two words, spelled the same but pronounced differently, are connected in this way. The Romans called minutes *Minuta Prima* The first small division of the hour. Then we divide it again, a second time, and they called these yet smaller periods of time *Minuta Secundum* The second small division of the hour, and these we call seconds.

    The Sumerians, who lived in Mesopotamia (present day Iraq), are usually credited with devising the sexagesimal counting system with a base of 60. The measurements of 60 seconds in a minute and 60 minutes in an hour were therefore devised in 4000 BC and remain the oldest unchanged method of measuring.

    Minutes can also be notes taken at a meeting that are usually written in shorthand or in an abbreviated small way before being written up in more detail later.

MIRROR Latin *Mirare* To wonder at.

MISSILE Latin *Missilis* To throw.

    The derivation is therefore from the act of launching the item rather than the object itself.

MODEM Derived from the first syllables of *Mod*ulator and *Dem*odulator. A modem is a device for connecting a computer and a telephone, a process that requires modulation of the signal suitable for transmission by an audio device and then demodulation when it arrives at the destination computer.

MODERN Latin *Modo* Just now, lately.

MONARCH Greek *Monos* Single and *Archein* To rule.
Rule by a single person.

MONDAY *See Days of the Week.*

MONEY Juno was the Roman Goddess of many things including all matters relating to the state and was, when acting in her capacity as guardian of the state finances, additionally known as Juno Moneta. The Roman mint was located in her temple.

MONOCLE Greek *Monos* Single and Latin *Oculus* Eye.
A monocle is a single lens to improve the sight of just one eye. A binocular Greek *Bi* Two and Latin *Oculus* Eye is the same thing for two eyes.

MONOPOLY Greek *Monos* Single and *Polein* To Sell.
A monopoly exists when a single person or company has exclusive rights to sell an item.

MONTHS OF THE YEAR

The names of the months are all of Greek or Latin derivation whereas the days of the week, with the exception of Saturday, are all northern European and Scandinavian. *See also Days of the Week.*

January: The first month of the year is dedicated to Janus the Roman god whose two heads enabled him to look both ways at once as he guarded doorways. Since a doorway often marks the beginning of a journey he also keeps watch over the beginning of the year.

February: Latin *Februum* Purification. The Februa purification ritual was held on 15th February just before the end of the year, since February was, until 450 BC, the final month of the year.

March: Named after Mars, the Roman god of war. He started as a protector of cattle and farmland but as the Roman empire expanded so too did his brief which eventually extended to include protecting the legions whose business was war. Originally the first month of the year.

April: Latin *Aprilis* To open. This derivation is uncertain but likely to be from the spring when flowers open.

May: Named after the Greek goddess of fertility, Maia, whose festival takes place at the time of year when many fertile animals produce their offspring.

June: Juno was the Roman goddess of marriage and it was considered particularly lucky to be married in her month. *See also Money.*

July: Formerly called *Quintilis* since it was the fifth month of the year when March was the first. It is commonly believed to have been renamed in honour of Julius Caesar who was born on 13 July 100 BC, however there is also evidence to suggest that this summer month was called *Jule* before the emperor was born and that the word was derived from *Huil* Wheel, the symbol of the summer solstice.

August: Re-named after the Emperor Augustus in 8 BC having been previously called *Sextilis*, the sixth month of the old calendar, which had 29 days. Not happy to be outdone by Julius Caesar, whose month had 31 days, legend has it that Augustus took two from February and added them to August, thus breaking the simple rule that alternate months had 30 and 31 days.

September: Latin *Septem* Seven. The seventh month of the old calendar.

October: Greek *Octo* Eight. The eighth month of the old calendar.

November: Latin *Novem* Nine. The ninth month of the old calendar.

December: Latin *Decem* Ten. The tenth month of the old calendar.

MOPED A *Mo*tor assisted *Ped*al Cycle.
The first mopeds were powered by a combination of motor and pedal power.

MORGANATIC German *Morgengabe* Morning gift.
A morganatic marriage is one in which people of differing social rank are required to accept that their children have no rights of succession to the higher ranking parent's titles, hereditary position and property, etc. The 'morning gift' was a token gift given to a bride by a husband on the morning following their wedding and, in the case of a morganatic marriage, represented the only obligation to her and any children they might have.

MORPHINE Greek *Morpheus* The God of dreams.
Morpheus was the brother of Hypnos, the God of Sleep (from whom we derive hypnosis) and Nyx, the Goddess of Night. Morphine, the pain-relieving drug that induces relaxation and possibly dreams, is named after Morpheus. *See also Heroin.*

MORRIS DANCING Latin *Mauri* The tribe that inhabited the Roman province of Mauretania.
When the Moors, as they became known, were expelled

from Spain in 1492 celebrations known as *Morescas* were held throughout the country and in some areas they still are. The folk dances we call Morris dancing, characterised by the hitting of sticks, waving handkerchiefs and bells sewn onto clothing, were performed at these events before spreading throughout Europe. *See also Gibraltar and Tariff.*

MORSEL Latin *Morsus* A bite.

A small bite-sized piece of anything.

MORTAR Latin *Mortarium* The vessel in which Roman builders mixed sand and cement.

Mortar became the word for the mixture itself and has also been retained as the word for a vessel in which substances are ground with a pestle. *See also Pestle.*

MORTGAGE Old French *Mort* Death and *Gage* A Pledge.

A mortgage is a loan agreement that remains in place until the loan is dead or in other words repaid.

MOSAIC Named after Moses who dictated that the breastplates of high priests be divided into twelve squares, each of a different colour. Hence inlaid work of different coloured stones is called mosaic work.

MUFFIN Old French *Moufflet* Soft.

MUGGY Welsh *Mwygl* Tepid, sultry.

MULLED Old Norman *Molda* To bury.

Ale given at funerals was always warmed and was called *molde* ale or funeral ale. Later any warmed ale or wine became known as mulled.

MULLIGATAWNY Tamil *Milagu* Pepper and *Tannir* Water.
   The soup originated in Tamil-speaking Sri Lanka and southern India and consists of ingredients produced there such as rice, noodles and turmeric.

MUMBO-JUMBO Mandingo (central West Africa) *Mama Dyumbo* An idol worshipped by certain African tribes.
   Christian colonists, obviously considering the idol to be false, considered the practice nonsensical, thus the term *Mumbo-jumbo* has become synonymous with any kind of nonsense.

MUMMY Persian *Mum* Wax.
   Wax plays an important part in the process of embalming Egyptian mummies.

MUM'S THE WORD The word 'mum' is produced with closed lips, and therefore indicates a necessity for silence. Thus the phrase '*Mum's the word*' is often said after a secret has been shared, or when something needn't be said. It has nothing to do with mothers.

MUSEUM Greek *Mousa* Muse.
   The Muses were a group of Greek goddesses who inspired all branches of the arts. Hence museums, the modern-day custodians of the arts, are named after them. *See also Music.*

MUSHROOM French *Mousseron* A plant that grows in the forest among the moss or *mousse*. The French call the mushroom *champignon* a plant that grows in the fields or *champs*.

MUSIC Greek *Mousa* Muse.
   The Muses most associated with music were Polyhymnia and Terpsichore. Given that they all have a Greek origin, it is very likely that the music-related words polyphonic, hymn, chord,

chorus and harpsichord are all derived from the names of these two Muses. The muses were goddesses who promoted the arts. *See also Museum.*

MUSLIN Muslim dress was often composed of muslin, a light cotton fabric well-suited to the hot climates of the Near- and Middle East. When it was first imported to England in 1670 it was given the name, albeit the phonetic name, of the people who had created it.

NAPKIN Old French *Nappe* Tablecloth and Middle English *Kin* Small.

A napkin is a miniature tablecloth for personal use. *See also Map.*

NARCISSUS The Flower. Greek *Narke* Numbness.

The plant has a sedative effect and thus derives from the same Greek root as Narcotic. In Greek mythology Narcissus was a beautiful young man who fell in love with his own reflection on the surface of a pond and killed himself when his approaches were not reciprocated.

NARK Romany *Nak* Nose.

A nark is someone who sticks his nose into other people's business, such as police informers, otherwise known as copper's narks.

NASTY Finnish *Naski* Pig.

The word is an allusion to the supposedly filthy habits of pigs. In Danish *Smaské* is to eat like pig and in Swedish *Snaskig* means filthy. But as any farmer will tell you the pig's attention to matters of personal hygiene in their sties shows that, at the very least, this is inappropriate.

NAVVY Labourers who undertook the immense task of building Britain's navigation canals were nick-named navvies and the name is still used for any manual worker.

NAZI An abbreviation of *Nationalsozialist*, in turn abbreviated from *Nationalsozialistische Deutsche Arbeiterpartei*, (National Socialist German Workers' Party) the political party led by Hitler. *See also Fascist.*

NEANDERTHAL German *Neander* and *Thal* Valley.
The first evidence of Neanderthals was discovered in the Neander Valley, east of Dusseldorf. *See also Dollar.*

NECTARINE Persian *Nectarine* Perfect.
A nectarine was considered to be the perfect peach. The word does not share an origin with Nectar as that is Greek *Nec* Death and *Tar* Overcoming. Being the food of the Gods it is the fare of those who have overcome death. *See also Peach.*

NEIGHBOUR Old English *Neah* Near and *Gebur* A farmer.
A reference to the days when pretty well everyone worked on the land and so all neighbours were farmers.

NEOLITHIC Greek *Neo* New and *Lithos* Stone.
The Neolithic people lived in the New Stone Age commencing 10,000 BC.

NEPOTISM Latin *Nepos* Grandson and Italian *Nepotismo* Nephew.
Nepotism originally referred to the habit of popes granting undue favouritism to young members of their own families but now applies to the same practice regardless of the position of the person who grants the favour.

NEUTER Latin *Ne* Not and *Uter* Either.
A neutered animal is not either gender.

NICKEL German *Nickel* Deceitful.

In German the malleable silvery metal is called *Kupfernicke* from *Kuper* Copper and *Nickel* Deceitful. The derivation is on account of the similarity in appearance of nickel and copper ore, which deceived miners into believing they had found the latter when in fact they had not.

NICOTINE Named after John Nicot (1530–1600) who introduced tobacco to France in 1560.

NIGHTINGALE Anglo-Saxon *Niht* Night and *Galan* To sing.

Though the nightingale sings throughout the day, its song can be better heard at night when other birds are silent.

NISI Latin *Nisi* If not.

A 'decree nisi' is a court ruling that has no force if specified conditions are not met. Only when they are met does it become a 'decree absolute'.

NITWIT Variations of no and none appear in most European languages No, Non, Nix, Niet, Nein so *Nit* means No and English *Wit* Intelligence. A nitwit is therefore a person devoid of intelligence.

NOB This slang word for nobles originated with the habit of their sons writing *fil. nob.*, meaning 'son of a noble', after their names in college registers. *See also Snob.*

NOOK Gaelic *Nuic* A corner.

The word that is so often coupled with nook, a cranny, comes from an old French word *Cran* A Fissure. The expression 'nooks and crannies' must therefore have been devised in English after the two words arrived here from different origins.

NOON Latin *Nona hora*. The ninth hour of the day.

Noon was originally two hours later, the ninth hour being 2.00pm or nine hours after 5.00am at which hour monastic life commenced. Noon was the hour at which monks took a break for a meal but when it became common practice to eat the midday meal earlier the term noon moved as well. With this new definition came the unsubstantiated folk etymology that after the clock strikes the number twelve there are no more numbers, none or *noon*, to count until the number one, after which the sequence begins again. So Noon or Mid-day was the hour thought to have no number but the former derivation is perhaps more plausible.

NORTH Indo-European *Ner* Left.

North is to the left when facing the rising sun. *See also East, South, and West.*

NOSE Anglo-Saxon *Ness* A prominence.

We still use the word unchanged from the original in the names of geographical promontories such as Sheerness and Shoeburyness. The word Nostril is also Saxon, from *Ness Thyrell*, referring to the holes, which look as though they have been bored with an auger.

NOSH Yiddish *Nāsh* Snack and German *Naschen* To nibble.

NOVEMBER *See Months of the Year.*

NUCLEUS Latin *Nucis* A nut.

A nucleus lies at the centre of something just as the kernel of a nut lies at the centre of its woody shell.

NUMBERS The English names for numbers 1 to 999,999 are all of Anglo-Saxon origin but the word million comes through

French, from Latin. Similarly all ordinals, those words that describe a position such as first, second, third etc, are Anglo-Saxon with the sole exception of second, which is of French origin. This is because the Anglo-Saxons counted first, other, third, fourth etc. Since other had an alternative meaning, the word second was introduced to clarify the situation. Second originally comes from the Latin *Sequor* to follow, the number that follows one, and is derived from the same root as 'sequential'.

NURSE Latin *Nutrix* To nourish.

To nurse a child is to suckle it for nourishment. Later a nurse was anyone who cared for or nourished a person in need of help.

NUTMEG French *Noix muscade* Scented nut.

The nutmeg is the fruit of the *Myristaca moschata* tree, a native of the Molucca Islands and has a distinctive aroma.

OAF Norwegian *Alfr* A silly person.

OBAMA Dholuo (The language of the Luo tribe of Kenya.) *O* He and *Bama* Slightly bent, but we hasten to add as in angular rather than corrupt. *See also Barack.*

OBELISK Greek *Obelos* A spit.
An obelisk, as in a tall pillar, resembles the shape of a spit used in cooking.

OBITUARY Latin *Obituarius* On the way to meet one's ancestors.
Death was as taboo a subject for the Romans as it is for many people today. Thus we have many expressions that avoid use of the word death such as 'passed away' or 'fallen asleep' and, in a similar way, the Romans said that they had gone to meet their ancestors.

OBLIVION Latin *Oblivisci* To forget.
Oblivion refers to the total eradication of something from memory.

OBNOXIOUS Latin *Noxa* Injury.
Obnoxious behaviour used to refer to an action that exposed

people to injury but now it tends only to refer to behaviour so
dreadful that it might lead to injured feelings.

OBSCURE Greek *Skeue* Covering.
A covering renders an item obscure.

OBSEQUIOUS Latin *Sequi* To follow.
Obsequiousness is an over-willingness to follow someone in a
servile manner.

OBSTREPEROUS Latin *Strepere* To shout.
To be obstreperous is to shout and make a lot of noise,
particularly in resistance of authority.

OBSTRUCT Latin *Structum* To build.
To construct is to build. Something which is counterproductive
to, or against progress, is to obstruct.

OCTOBER *See Months of the Year.*

OCTOPUS Greek *Octo* Eight and *Pous* Foot.
An octopus has eight legs which are quite different to the
tentacles found in other marine species.

ODD Old Norse *Oddi* The third number.
In Norse Oddi also means the point of a spear or sword.

OIL Greek *Elaion* An olive tree.
The olive was the principal source of oil.

O.K. American slang. An abbreviation of 'oll korrect'. It was a
common fad in the mid-nineteenth century, especially in
New York and Boston, for people to spell words based on
the way they sounded and abbreviate them accordingly.

O.K. was originally O.W., standing for 'oll wright'. Several other acronyms arose around the same time, including N.S. ('nuff said'), but none of these have survived as well or spread so widely as OK which has now infiltrated virtually every language in the world.

OMBUDSMAN Old Scandinavian *Umbodsmann* Representative.
An ombudsman represents the interests of the people against those who govern.

OMELETTE Latin *Lamella* A thin layer.
An omelette is prepared by frying a thin layer of egg in a thin layer of oil. The word laminate derives from the same root.

OPAL Polish *Opalać* To burn on all sides, from *Palać* To glow.
The opal, when exposed to light, could be said to glow from all sides.

OPEN SESAME Arabic *Simsim* Sesame.
The seedpods of the sesame burst open when they reach maturity; hence Ali Baba famously spoke the words so that the mouth of the treasure cave would burst open and admit him. The sesame seed also has mythological associations with immortality and witchcraft.

OPIUM Greek *Opos* Sap.
Opium is obtained from the sap of a poppy.

ORANGE Sanskrit *Naranj* Orange.
The fruit entered English vernacular as 'a Naranj'. Hearing this aloud, it is understandable how it was gradually corrupted to 'an Orange'.

ORANGUTAN Malay, Indonesian *Orang* Person and *Hutan* Forest.

The highly intelligent orangutan, the largest animals to live in trees, were considered persons from the forest.

ORCHID Greek *Orchis* Testicle.

The plant is named because of the similarity of shape between its tubers and a testicle. There are in excess of 20,000 species of orchid one of which is Vanilla. *See also Avocado and Vanilla.*

OREGANO Greek *Oros* Mountain and *Ganos* Brightness.

The name refers to the bright purple flowers of the oregano plant and its mountainous natural habitat.

ORIGAMI Japanese *Ori* Folding and *Kami* Paper.

The art of folding paper to resemble birds and flowers originated in Japan.

OUIJA French *Oui* Yes and German *Ja* Yes.

The boards with letters and a pointing device used in a séance are therefore Yes-Yes boards, that being the usual answer to the question 'Is there anyone there?'

PACIFIC Latin *Pax* Peace and *Facere* To make.

In 1520 after passing through the straits at the southernmost part of South America that would later bear his name, Ferdinand Magellan, the Portuguese explorer, headed north-west into the Pacific Ocean sailing for three months and twenty days before coming across land. He found the weather so fair and the winds so favourable that he named the body of water the *pacifique*, the peaceful ocean. *See also Patagonia.*

PAGAN Latin *Paganus* Villager.

The spread of Christianity in the Roman Empire was slower in the country than in the cities. Hence those outside the cities, the *paganii*, were likely to be unbelievers and followers of more primitive folk traditions. *See also Heathen.*

PAIN Latin *Poena* Penalty.

It was believed that suffering pain was the penalty for having committed a sin.

PAL Romany *Pal* Brother.

PALACE Latin *Collis Palatinus* Palatine Hill.

The most central of the seven hills on which the city of Rome is built, the Palatine Hill is the site of the cave where the she-wolf suckled the abandoned Romulus and Remus and where the former created the first Roman settlement that was named after him. From about 500 BC Emperors built their palaces on the hill, which overlooked the Circus Maximus on one side and the Forum on the other. The word palace is derived from that original location, the Palatine Hill, as is the adjective Palatial. *See also Suburb.*

PALL MALL   Italian *Pallamaglio* Mallet ball.
A game in which a wooden ball was struck through one of two iron hoops set up at either end of an alley and the player who achieved this with the least strokes was the winner. When, in the early seventeenth century, the game was introduced to London it was first played in an alley near St James's Street, later to be known as Pall Mall, a corrupted name of the game. Later still the game ceased to be popular and the streets became shopping centres and the expression shopping mall was born.

PAMPHLET   French *Par un filet* By a thread.
A pamphlet is a booklet with the pages stitched together with a piece of thread.

PANAMA HAT   These wide-brimmed straw hats are made in Ecuador not Panama. During the construction of the Panama Canal, that opened in 1914, so many of the workers suffered from the heat that they were issued with hats brought in from Ecuador. When asked where their hats came from after they returned home they replied: 'Panama'.

PANE   A pane, as in a pane of glass, is a contraction of the word panel.

PANIC Pan was a general who, being surrounded by an opposing army while camped one night in a valley, ordered his men to shout. The sound echoed around the hills, increasing in volume so much that the enemy fled fearing a much greater opposing force than there actually was. Hence groundless fear is known as panic.

PANNIER Latin *Panis* Bread.
Panniers are baskets for carrying bread. While originally they would be suspended from either side of a pack animal's back, they are now more frequently seen on bikes and motorcycles.

PANSY Greek *Panacea* All healing.
It was believed that the pansy plant was a cure for all known diseases. The English also noticed the plant's medicinal qualities as a cure for sorrow and called it Heart's-ease.

PANTRY Latin *Panis* Bread.
A pantry was originally the room where bread was kept.

PAPER Greek *Papyros*.
The Egyptian reed of that name grows in the marshes of the Nile delta and, when pulped, produces a soft pith from which early paper was made. *See also Library.*

PAPIER MÂCHÉ *Paper* and Latin *Masticatus* Chewed.
Papier mâché is a paper that has been pulped, or chewed, before being pasted together.

PAPOOSE Algonquin (Central North America around the Great Lakes and eastern Canada) *Papoos* Child.
It refers to a native American child of any tribal origin.

PARACHUTE Italian *Parare* To defend and French *Chute* To fall.
Parachutes are described in Chinese texts from AD 500 and a
thousand years later in Europe most famously by Leonardo da
Vinci. In the absence of aeroplanes they were mostly used to
escape from burning buildings.

PARAFFIN Latin *Para* Little and *Affinis* Affinity.
Paraffin, or paraffin wax, is unusual in having little similarity or
affinity with other chemicals. In America it is called Kerosene,
which is derived from Greek *Keros* Wax.

PARANOIA Greek *Para* Beyond and *Noos* The mind.
Paranoia is a mental disorder exhibiting characteristics beyond
the normal processes of the mind.

PARAPHERNALIA Greek *Para* Beyond and *Pherne* Dowry.
The word originally described any possessions brought by a
woman into a marriage that were not classed as dowry and
thus remained her property as opposed to becoming her
husband's. Perhaps it was the latter who turned the word into
a derogatory term for unwanted and miscellaneous articles.
See also Trousseau.

PARASITE Sanskrit *Paraasritahah* and Greek *Parasitos* One who is
dependent on another, or who lives at another's expense.

PARENT Latin *Parere* To bring forth.

PARKA Aleut *Parqua* Skin.
A parka is a hooded jacket similar to an anorak and made
originally from skins. Aleut is the language of the inhabitants
of the Aleutian Islands that stretch in a long line from the south

of Alaska across the north Pacific towards the Kamchatka Peninsula. Also in the Nenets vocabulary, a language spoken in eastern Siberia. *See also Anorak.*

PARLIAMENT French *Parler* To speak.

The French described meetings of their State assembly as a *parlement* in the mid-twelfth century. The first English parliament met on 22 January 1265. The shortest lasted for one day in 1399 in order to depose Richard II and the longest from 1640 until dissolved by Cromwell in 1653.

PARSNIP Latin *Pastinum* Forked and Anglo-Saxon *Næpe* Neep.

A parsnip is a neep, a Scots word for a root vegetable such as the swedes traditionally served with haggis and tatties on Burns night. A parsnip frequently forks to end in two points. *See also Turnip.*

PARVENU French *Pervenir* To attain.

A parvenu is someone who has attained a social standing through the acquisition of wealth and position but still is considered an upstart.

PASS Latin *Passus* A step.

To pass by anything you need to move one step at a time.

PASTA Latin *Pasta* Dough.

PASTOR Latin *Pascere* To feed.

A pastor cares for his congregation as a mother cares for and feeds her child.

PASTURE Latin *Pascere* To feed.

A pasture is where animals feed.

PATAGONIA Spanish *Patagon* Big feet.

When the explorer Ferdinand Magellan (1480–1521) visited the southern tip of South America before rounding the cape and becoming the first European to sail across the Pacific, he noticed that the natives were, on average, 10 inches (25cms) taller than his crew and therefore had very large feet. *See also Pacific.*

PATHETIC Greek *Pathetikos* Sensitive, capable of emotion.

PAWN Spanish *Peone* A foot soldier.

A pawn is the smallest piece on the chess board, that row of foot soldiers that protect the important pieces behind them. It can also be used in the sense of someone who plays a mere supporting role in some aspect of life.

PEACH Latin *Pesca* Peach, from *Malum Persica* Persian apple.

The peach, though native to China, came to Europe via Ancient Persia. *See also Nectarine.*

PEARL BARLEY A corruption of peeled barley, that is barley without its outer shell or husk.

PEDIGREE Old French *Pe de gru* Crane's foot.

The connecting lines on a family tree resemble the widely splayed claws of a crane's foot. *See also Geranium.*

PEN Latin *Penna* A feather.

The first writing implements were made from reeds in Egypt 5000 years ago. In the Middle Ages they were replaced by quill pens, which were made from the large feathers of geese or, better still, swans. Pen knives are so-named because they were used to shape the feathers for quill pens. Somewhat confusingly an adult female swan is also called a pen, but this derived from Welsh *Pynne* Loud.

PENINSULA   Latin *Pene* Almost and *Insula* An island.
So a peninsula, a strip of land barely attached to the mainland, was thought of as being almost an island.

PENTHOUSE French *Appentis,* from Latin *Appendicum* An appendage.
A penthouse is a separate part of a building, usually a luxury flat, that was often added as a later appendage.

PERFUME   Latin *Per* and *Fumus* Smoke.
Perfumes were originally scents derived from burning flowers, spices and essential oils.

PERISCOPE   Greek *Periskopeein* To look around.

PERIWINKLE   Anglo-Saxon *Petty* Small and *Wincle* Shell-fish.

PESTLE   Old English *Pestle* The leg of an animal, usually a pig.
The grinder used in a mortar was originally made from a leg-bone. *See also Mortar.*

PETRIFY   Latin *Petra* Rock and *Facere* To make.
To petrify is to make into stone. This can be either literal, via the long geological process, or figuratively, as in the temporary, rock steady paralysis induced by being extremely scared.

PETROLEUM   Latin *Petra* Rock and *Oleum* Oil.
The crude oil from which petrol is made occurs naturally in rock formations, however the name is misleading since it

is not, as the name suggests, distilled from the rock itself. Equally inaccurate is the American term for the same substance gasoline since it is a liquid and not a gas.

PHARMACY Greek *Pharmakon* A drug.

PHEASANT Greek *Phasianos* Phasian.
These ornate birds, though found nowadays throughout the world, are named after the Phasis River in the Kingdom of Colchis where they were first encountered. Colchis was in present day Georgia and the river, which flows into the Black Sea, is now called the Rioni River.

PHILOSOPHER Greek *Phile* A lover of and *Sophia* Wisdom.

PHONEY Gaelic *Fainne* Ring.
In the nineteenth century swindlers sold gilt brass rings to recently arrived Irish immigrants telling them they were real gold.

PHOTOGRAPHY Greek *Photos* Light and *Graphein* To draw.

PISTOL Pistols were first shipped to England in 1526 from Pistoia, Tuscany, where the handheld gun was invented for use on horseback.

PLACEBO Latin *Placebo* I shall please.
A placebo is a type of treatment that will do nothing for the patient other than give him peace of mind. It is made to look like the real thing but in reality is often no more than a sugar pill. A doctor prescribing it for psychological benefit, as opposed to its other use as a control in testing drugs, might therefore say 'This will not provide any cure but it will please him'.

PLANET Greek *Planetes* To wander.

> Before the discoveries by early astronomers such as Galileo (1564–1642), who proved that the planets circled the sun, and Kepler (1571–1630), who showed that their orbits were elliptical, it was thought that planets wandered aimlessly through space rather than taking clearly defined routes.

PLANTAGENET The name of the royal house that provided England with monarchs from 1154 to 1485 was first adopted by the Counts of Anjou after the first Count caused himself to be scourged as penance for some crime he had committed by being beaten with branches of broom plant *Planta Genesta*. Geoffrey Count of Anjou was father of the first Plantagenet king, Henry II (1154–1189).

PLASTER OF PARIS Greek *Plassein* To mould.

> This material was first imported to England from a gypsum mine at Montmartre in Paris.

PLASTIC Greek *Plassein* To mould.

> Plastic originally referred to an object's pliability, or plasticity, however the word is now much more widely used to describe things that have already been moulded into a shape.

PLUMMET Latin *Plumbum* Lead.

> Early builders used lumps of lead on strings called plumb lines or plumb bobs to check that constructions were vertical. Any weight on a string will plummet downwards.

PLUNDER Dutch *Plunderen* To steal household goods.

POACHER French *Poche* Pocket, bag.

> A poacher is one who unlawfully kills and pockets another

man's game, likewise, a poached egg is so-called because in boiling water, the white forms a pocket around the yolk.

POETRY Greek *Poieo* To create and *Poiesis* Imaginative.
Creative and imaginative use of the language. The word originally had no connection with rhyme or metre.

POLICE Latin *Politia* Civil administration, from Greek *Polis* City.

POLO Tibetan *Pulu* Ball.
Polo is a ball game played on horseback, in the water and occasionally on elephants and bicycles.

POM Australian slang *POME* Prisoner of Mother England.
It is believed that deported prisoners arriving in Australia had these initials printed on their shirts.

PONG Romany *Pan* To stink.

PONZI A ponzi scheme, named after the swindler Charles Ponzi (1882–1949), is a fraud perpetrated when investors are paid interest derived from the capital of people making investments after them rather than from interest earned on their own savings. These pyramid selling scams can be made to look very attractive in a rising market but invariably collapse when returns fall. The most notable ponzi scam is that of Bernard Madoff who swindled investors out of $65 billion before it was exposed in 2008.

PORCELAIN Italian *Porcellana* A cowrie shell.
The delicate shell-like surface of porcelain resembles the smooth surface of a cowrie. Porcelain is also known as China since, before 1600, that country was the only producer and so, like so many other early imports, it took its name from its place of origin.

PORCUPINE Latin *Porcus* A pig and *Spina* A spine.

A porcupine was considered to be a pig with spines. In fact they are in the rodent family. *See also Rodent.*

PORPOISE French *Porc* Hog and *Poisson* Fish.

It is curious that while the English call the animal by a French name, the French have adopted an Anglo-Saxon one: *mere-swine,* or sea-pig.

PORTCULLIS French *Porte* Gate, door and *Coleice* Sliding.

Entrances to large castles invariably had two portcullises. The enemy would be enticed into the castle through the open outer one, be stopped by the locked inner one only to be trapped there when the previously hidden outer one was slammed down behind them.

POST Latin *Positus* Placed.

The word 'post' is used in a variety of senses – post office, a post in the ground, a military posting, posting to a ledger – but an understanding of the root explains each one as a placement of something – a letter, a wooden pole, a person or some figures – in its appointed place.

POSTSCRIPT Latin *Post Scriptum* Written afterwards. A P.S.

POTATO Taino (West Indies) *Batata* Sweet potato and Quechua (Andean) *Papa* Potato.

Many European explorers, notably Sir Walter Raleigh (1552–1618) have been credited with introducing the potato to Europe from Haiti and the Bahamas, the islands they first came to having sailed across the Atlantic.

POULTICE Greek *Poltos* Porridge.

A poultice is a warm coating applied to a wound originally

made with foods such as porridge or bread. In the eighteenth century poultices were infused with lead. Such a mixture was administered to Beethoven in order to cure his distended abdomen, however it probably hastened his death.

PRAIRIE French *Prairie* Meadow, pasture land.
French settlers in America used the word to describe the endless plains they found there.

PRECOCIOUS Latin *Prae* Early and *Coquere* To cook or ripen.
A precocious child is one that is an early developer. A precocious fruit or vegetable is one that has ripened early. *See also Apricot.*

PREFACE Latin *Prae* Before and *Fatus* To speak.
A preface can therefore be a spoken introduction as well as the more accepted written form at the beginning of a book.

PREGNANT Latin *Prae* Before and *Gnasci* To be born.

PREJUDICE Latin *Prae* Before and *Judicium* Judgement.
Prejudice is a judgement made before the matter is judged upon in a court of law.

PREPOSTEROUS Latin *Præ* Before and *Posterus* After.
It is preposterous to place before that which should be after. The word therefore has the same meaning as the saying 'to put the cart before the horse'.

PROFIT Latin *Profectus* To make progress.

PROGNOSIS Greek *Pro* and *Gignoskein* To know.

PROGRAMME Greek *Programma.*

Before being presented to the Athenian senate for debate, proposed laws were published on tablets for inspection. At this stage it was therefore a plan or programme and not yet the final draft. A *programma* was similar to present day white papers issued to familiarise members of parliament with proposed legislation.

PROLETARIAT Latin *Proles* Offspring.

In ancient Rome the proletariat were the lowest of the six classes and comprised people who owned no property and whose only contribution to the state was to provide children.

PRONOUNCE *Pro* Forth and *Nuntius* A messenger.

PUFFIN Cornish. The puffin used to be found on most Cornish cliffs where for centuries they provided food and oil but now the colonies have tended to move further north to more productive feeding grounds. The Norse for Puffin is *Lund* hence Lundy off the coast of Devon is Puffin Island, but now the birds are seldom seen there either.

PUKKA Hindi *Pukka* Cooked or perfectly done.

Adapted throughout the British Empire to describe not just food but anything that is perfect, it is most frequently used to describe good people, as with the phrase *Pukka Sahib* meaning 'excellent fellow'.

PUNT Latin *Pons* Bridge.

From *pons* is derived the French *pontoon*, which in most European languages now signifies a flat-bottomed vessel used as a temporary floating bridge. The word punt, referring to a flat-bottomed boat, is a contraction of *pontoon.*

PUSS Ancient Gaelic *Puss* A cat.

PYGMY Greek *Pygmaeus* Dwarf.

As well as being applied to certain tribes in sub-Saharan Africa whose average height was appreciably less than that of the European explorers who discovered them, a pygmy was also a measure of length said to be the distance from the elbow to the knuckles of a small person defined as 13.5 inches (34.5 cms). *See also Elbow.*

PYJAMAS Persian *Payjama* Leg garment.

PYRRHIC A pyrrhic victory is one achieved with great loss to the victor. King Pyrrhus of Epirus defeated the Romans twice at Heraclea in 280 BC and at Asculum in the following year but his losses were so great that he commented 'One more battle like these and we will be totally undone'.

Q Latin *Cauda* A tail.

The letter Q is simply the letter O, but with a tail.

QUAFF Low German *Quassen* To overindulge, especially in food or drink.

QUAKER The Religious Society of Friends was founded in the mid-seventeenth century by George Fox, the son of a Leicestershire weaver, who was disillusioned with the existing Christian denominations. His supporters became known as Quakers after Fox exhorted a Derby magistrate to quake at the word of the Lord.

QUALM Old English *Cwealm* Disaster usually associated with the pain of the plague.

The word's current meaning, a state of unease, is moderate by comparison.

QUANDARY French *Qu'en dirai-je?* What shall I say of it?

The word is a corruption of this query, which seeks explanation for a puzzle or perplexity.

QUANGO *QU*asi *A*utonomous *N*on-*G*overnmental *O*rganisation.

An acronym to describe government-appointed bodies that operate away from mainstream government and are often ridiculed for lack of accountability and excessive expenditure.

QUARANTINE Latin *Quadraginta* Forty, the number of days of isolation necessary to prevent the spread of contagious diseases.

Ships entering harbour were required to fly a yellow flag to show if they were 'in quarantine', or a yellow and black one to indicate that a contagious disease was on board. The first astronauts returning from the moon also underwent a period of quarantine; however no similar precautions were made to prevent diseases from earth reaching space.

QUARREL Latin *Querula* To complain.

A quarrel was therefore the complaint of one party against another that led to a quarrelsome disagreement rather than altercation itself.

QUART Latin *Quartus* A fourth.

A quart is one fourth of a gallon.

QUICHE German *Kuchen* A cake.

The quiche originated in Lorraine, a region in the north-east of France where dialects of German are still spoken.

QUIZ Latin *Quaestio* To ask.

Probably from the same root as question. There is sadly no truth in the oft quoted suggestion that this strange word originates from a bet accepted by a Dublin theatre proprietor in 1790 that he could not introduce a new word into the language overnight. He persuaded friends to write 'Quiz' on walls all over the city so that in the morning everyone was seeking an explanation for this puzzling word. But sadly it cannot be true as the word was in use a century before.

RABBI Hebrew *Rabbi* My great one, or teacher.

RACE (As in nationality.) Mœso-Gothic *Raz* House.
We use this in the sense of the House of Israel or the House of Windsor, both of which have a strong connection to nationality.

RACKET Arabic *Rahat* The palm of the hand.
Many games now played with a racket – or racquet – once used the bare or gloved hand to strike the ball. In fives, however, a game similar to squash, the ball is still struck with a gloved hand.

RACKETEER In the seventeenth century, English pickpockets would cause a racket, or a loud noise, by throwing devices such as squibs and rockets in order to otherwise engage their victims' attention and allow them to steal undetected. *See also Whippersnapper.*

RADAR American acronym for *RA*dio *D*etecting *A*nd *R*ange-finding.
A term first used during the Second World War. The device was perfected for military use by Sir Robert Watson-Watt, a

descendent of James Watt the inventor of the steam engine. It is considered to have played a major role in winning the war.

RAMBLE Latin *Perambulo* To wander about.

RASCAL French *Racaille* Scum or rabble, from Norman-French *Rasque* Mud.

RATHER Old English *Hrathor* More quickly, sooner.
To say that one would *rather* do one thing over another is to say that one would *sooner* do that one thing over the other.

RAVIOLI Italian *Rava* Turnip.
A popular filling was originally puréed turnip.

RAVISH Latin *Rapere* and French *Ravir* To seize and carry off.

RECTOR Latin *Rectum* To rule.
A rector is someone appointed to a position of leadership, be it of a parish, a university, or in some cases, as headmaster of a school.

REFRIGERATE Latin *Re* From and *Frigus* Cold.
To refrigerate something is to change its temperature from one level to a colder one.

REGATTA Venetian *Regatta* An annual race between gondoliers.

REJUVENATE Latin *Juvenescere* To become young again.
To rejuvenate therefore means to return to a state of youthfulness, to reinvigorate. No cure for advancing years has yet been devised and so there is no word for literally becoming younger!

REPTILE Latin *Repere* To creep.

Most members of the class *Reptilia* snakes, lizards, crocodiles and alligators, creep along stealthily with their bodies close to the ground.

RETICENT Latin *Re* and *Tacere* To be silent.

Reticence, a reluctance to express oneself, is usually demonstrated as silence.

RETORT Latin *Torquere* To twist.

To retort is to turn an argument back on its originator, as if twisting its direction.

RHINOCEROS Greek *Rhinos* Nose and *Keras* Horn.

The distinctive horn on the noses of these ancient creatures gave rise to their name. The largest of the five remaining species, the African White Rhinoceros, second in size only to elephants as land animals, is not white at all but grey. The use of the word white in its name derives from Afrikaans *Wyd* Wide. The white rhinoceros has a wide lip, whereas the smaller black rhinoceros has a pointed lip. The black rhinoceros is grey as well but was termed black to distinguish it from the inappropriately named white rhinoceros.

RHODODENDRON Greek *Rhodos* Rose and *Dendron* Tree.

This Himalayan tree has rose-like flowers. The popularly held belief that the tree has a connection with the island of Rhodes is erroneous.

RIBALDRY *Rabod,* the seventh century heathen king of Friesland, is thought to be the derivation of this word. While standing in a pool awaiting baptism, he is said to have asked his Christian mentor, Bishop Wipan, where his forefathers had gone to. The response, as they had not been baptised, was that they had been sent to Hell, to which the king replied that he would rather spend eternity with his ancestors in Hell, than with a few Christian strangers in Heaven. This rejection of God was thought to be so vulgar and hateful that the king's name gradually came to be applied to anything deemed coarse or obscene.

RIDICULE Latin *Ridere* To laugh.
An expression of derision about an object or situation is often expressed with mocking laughter.

RIDING (As in the division of a county.) Norwegian *Tridjing* A third.
The county of Yorkshire is divided into three ridings, the North, the East and the West and the derivation explains why there is no South Riding.

RIFLE German *Reifeln* To form small grooves.
The firearm takes its name from spiral flutes in the barrel that cause the bullet to spin thus ensuring a straighter flight.

R. I. P. Latin *Requiescat in pace* May he or she rest in peace.

RIVAL Latin *Rivalis* One who shares a brook from *Rivus* A brook as in river.
The word originally referred to one of two people owning property on opposite sides of a brook both claiming exclusive ownership of the stream.

ROAM Italian *Romeo* A pilgrim going to Rome.
The word later became associated with vagrants who, despite their actual destination, would always say they were going

to Rome. From this we also get the saying, 'All roads lead to Rome'.

ROBOT Czech *Robota* Work, labour.
This word was first used by Czech writer Karel Čapek in his 1921 play 'Rossum's Universal Robots'. It was about artificial men that were manufactured to perform hard labour and explored the idea, as they could think and feel just as humans did, that they were being exploited.

RODENT Latin *Rodere* To gnaw.
Rodents have sharp incisor teeth that continue to grow throughout their lives and are kept short by constant gnawing. *See also Rostrum.*

ROMANCE When, in the ninth century, the French language began to replace that of the Romans as France's main vernacular, early tales of chivalry and romance such as *Beowulf* and *King Arthur* were still recounted in Latin or, more accurately, in a bad Latin dialect which became known as *Romance*. The term therefore became interchangeable with the genre, one of knights, princesses, magic and fantasy.

ROSEMARY Latin *Ros* Dew and *Marinus* Sea.
The rosemary plant is native to the rocky coasts of southern France and Italy where the early morning dew clings to its silvery grey leaves.

ROSTRUM Latin *Rostrum* Ship's prow, from *Rodere* To gnaw.
The Romans applied the term to the bow of a boat, which was fitted with sharp irons for the attacking or gnawing into an enemy ship. It was also applied to the orator's stage in their *forum* because of its resemblance to the prow of a ship. *See also Rodent.*

ROUNDHEAD This term of contempt applied to the Puritans at the time of the Civil War was derived from their custom of cutting their hair close to the head, which was in total contrast to the Royalists who wore their hair in elaborate ringlets.

ROUTINE French *Route* A road.
Hence a routine is the metaphorical practice of travelling down a well-defined road.

ROVER Dutch *Roover* A robber and Danish *Röverskip* A pirate ship.

RUBICON The *Rubicon* is a small river that once marked the border between Italy and Gaul that due to a treaty Roman generals were forbidden to cross. When Julius Cæsar did so in 49 BC, it caused a violent civil war. Hence to 'cross the Rubicon' is to embark on a rash and irrevocable act.

RUGBY William Webb Ellis (1806–1872) was credited with the invention of this game when, during a football match at Rugby School, he picked up the ball and ran with it. A plaque at the school records the event thus: 'This stone commemorates the exploit of William Webb Ellis who, with a fine disregard for the rules of football as played in his time, first took the ball in his arms and ran with it thus originating the distinctive feature of the rugby game AD 1823'. The William Webb Ellis Trophy is now awarded to the winner of The Rugby World Cup. *See also Cricket and Soccer.*

RUM DEAL There was a practice among booksellers in the eighteenth century of sending books to the plantations of the West Indies in exchange for barrels of rum. However, due to their customers' isolation from British culture they often seized on this arrangement as an opportunity to get rid of titles that did not sell well in England. Hence the phrase rum deal, refers to a deal in which one party does not receive a fair deal.

RUSTIC Latin *Rusticus* The country.

A rustic is therefore someone from the countryside. To be rusticated is to be banished to the countryside from a university.

S

SABOTAGE Turkish *Shabata* Galosh via French *Sabot* Wooden shoe. French peasants fearful that their livelihoods were threatened by the introduction of machinery used to throw their wooden shoes into the mechanism to cause damage. Later striking railway workers removed the 'shoes' that held railway lines in place and became known as saboteurs. The flat Italian *ciabatta* bread named after the Italian for slipper also derives from *Shabata*.

SADDLE Anglo-Saxon *Sadle* Seat.
Settles, the long, high-backed wooden seats found in farmhouses and pubs are derived from the same root.

SAFARI Arabic *Safara* Travel.

SAGO Malay *Sagu* A species of palm, the pith of which is processed to extract the starch that is used as a thickening agent in puddings.

SALAD Latin *Sal* Salt.
In ancient Rome it was customary to eat vegetable leaves with a lot of salt. Hence the dish that is nowadays associated with healthy eating has a name that derives from a substance now

associated with quite the opposite when used to excess. Salami
is similarly derived from the Latin for salt. *See also Sausage.*

SALARY Latin *Salarium* Salt money.

Roman soldiers were originally paid in salt as it was considered
to be a vital yet scarce food. Payment with salt was later
replaced by money with which to buy it and this was called
salt money or *salarium*. *See also Soldier and Wage.*

SALUTE Latin *Salus* Health.

Originally a salute as a greeting was an enquiry after someone's
health. It was much the same as our semi-automatic greeting
'How are you?' The military salute originated at jousting
tournaments when the winner shielded his eyes from the
bright light that was supposedly radiating from the lady or
senior person who presented the prize. Military salutes are
always carried out with outstretched fingers showing that
the hand holds no weapon. Finally a military salute with guns
firing blanks or purposely aimed in some safe direction shows
that there is no hostile intent and therefore respect for the
person in whose honour the salute is fired.

SAMBA Portuguese *Zamparse* To bump and crash.

This type of dance is always set to lively music and drums.
Although introduced into Europe from Brazil when that was
a Portuguese colony, the dance originated in Africa and was
carried across the Atlantic by slaves.

SAMBUCA Arabic *Sambuq* A type of ship used to import the
aniseed-flavoured alcoholic drink.

SAMPAN Mandarin *Sam* Three and *Pan* Plank.

A sampan has the simplest of constructions. A flat board for
the bottom and another to form either side of the boat.

SANDWICH John Montagu, The 4th Earl of Sandwich (1718–1792) asked that his meals to be brought to him between two slices of bread, so that he could eat without having to either leave or make a mess of his gaming table. A more generous explanation is that he worked so hard after his appointment as First Lord of the Admiralty that he seldom left his desk and asked that his food be brought to him as sandwiches in his office so that he could continue directing the British navy without a pause.

SANGRIA Spanish *Sangria* Bleeding.
Made with red wine, orange juice, and brandy, this traditional Spanish drink is so called because of its deep red colour.

SANITATION Latin *Sanitus* Health.
The Romans recognised that there was a strong connection between sanitation systems and good health. The Cloaca Maxima sewage system, a large drain flowing through Rome, was constructed in about 600 BC and continued to drain marshland and convey sewage to the River Tiber for 1000 years and may still be seen today.

SAPPER Latin *Sappa* A pick.
A sapper is a military engineer whose duties were originally to gain access to the enemy's position by digging trenches and tunnels with picks and shovels. Here they would undermine and destroy the fortifications to help their colleagues advance. To sap, from the same source, means to weaken.

SATIN Chinese *Zaytun* A seaport on the south-east coast of China, also known as Quanzhou, which was the world's largest during the Yuan Dynasty (1279–1368). Satin, a closely woven, glossy fabric, was first made in China and then exported by Arab traders through the port of *Zaytun*, from which it derived its name.

SATURDAY *See Days of the Week.*

SAUCER Latin *Salsa* Sauce.
Saucers were originally used alone as table dishes for sauces and salt. Their association with tea cups is a more recent innovation.

SAUNA Finnish *Savna* Bath.
The practice of pouring water onto hot stones to create very hot steam takes its name from an older term from the Sami language *suovdnji* meaning a depression in the snow created to give protection to a person or an animal. The Samis, frequently known as Lapps, a term they consider uncomplimentary, occupy the northern coastal regions of Scandinavia and western Russia.

SAUSAGE Latin *Salsus* Salted.
The sausage was invented 5000 years ago by the Sumerians in present day Iraq. However the name derives from the Roman practice of stuffing salted meat into animal intestines as a means of preserving it. *See also Salad.*

SAVAGE French *Sauvage* from Latin *Silva* Forest, grove.
To be savage is to act as though one is from the wild.

SAVVY Latin *Sapere* To be wise or knowing.
To be tech-savvy is to be knowledgeable about, and competent with, technology.

SCALLYWAG Irish *Sgaileog* Farm labourer.
The term is now most frequently used in English towns that have a high proportion of people of Irish descent.

SCAMP Latin *Ex* From and *Campus* Field.

A scamp originally described a soldier who absented himself from the battlefield. More recently it has been used to describe mischievous little boys.

SCAMPI Italian *Scampo* A shrimp.

The species of shrimp that is supposedly used to prepare scampi is also known as the Norway Lobster or the Dublin Bay Prawn. So it is a puzzle why we use the Mediterranean name when others from our own waters are available. Perhaps it sounds more exotic.

SCANDAL Greek *Scandalon* A stumbling block.

Scandals can certainly prove to be a stumbling block to both the private and professional lives of those whose secrets are exposed.

SCARLET Latin *Carnis* Flesh, through Italian *Scarlatino* Flesh-coloured.

SCENT French *Sentir* To smell.

It is not known why the silent 'c' was added.

SCHEDULE Latin *Schedula* A strip of paper. Originally any piece of paper such as a schedule might be written on.

SCIENCE Latin *Sciens* Knowing.

SCISSORS Latin *Scindere* To split.

Scissors is one of the few nouns in English that has no singular.

SCORE Old Norse *Skor* Notch.

An early way of recording a score of points in a game or kills in battle was to carve a notch in a tally stick.

SCOUNDREL Anglo-French *Escoundre* To hide oneself.
A scoundrel is someone who lurks in the shadows and operates among the criminal underclass of a society.

SCRUTINY Latin *Scruta* Rags.
This term referred to rag-and-bone men, whose work demanded that they scrutinise even old rags thoroughly because they were able to use materials that would otherwise be rejected as being valueless.

SCUFFLE Swedish *Skuffa* To push.
Scuffles invariably result in people pushing each other.

SCULPTOR Latin *Sculptum* To carve.

SCUPPER Old French *Escopir* To spit out.
The word was originally used to refer to the drainage holes in the side of ships intended to let out water. A scupper therefore saves a ship from sinking. But curiously as a verb it means to deliberately destroy a plan or an item. Therefore it would be acceptable to report the sinking of a ship by saying 'The ship was scuppered because someone blocked the scuppers'.

SECOND Latin *Secundus* To follow.
Second is the number that follows the first. *See also Minute and Numbers.*

SEDGE Anglo-Saxon *Sæcg* Sword.
The plant has little sword-like leaves. *See also Gladiator and Gladiola.*

SEDUCE Latin *Seducere* To lead.
Seduction involves leading someone in a particular direction and invariably leading them astray.

SEGREGATE Latin *Se* Apart and *Gregis* A flock.

Segregation is the setting apart of a person or an item from a larger group or flock. *See also Congregate and Gregarious.*

SEPIA Greek *Sepia* A cuttlefish.

These marine creatures are cephalopods in the same class as squid and octopuses and, as a defence mechanism, they eject clouds of opaque ink which can also be used as a sepia dye.

SEPTEMBER *See Months of the Year.*

SERENADE Spanish, Italian *Serenata,* from Latin *Serenus* Calm and Italian *Sera* Evening.

Originally a serenade was music played out of doors on a serene evening.

SERIOUS Old English *Swaere* from Latin *Serius* Gloomy.

A serious matter can often be a gloomy one.

SERPENT Latin *Serpere* To creep.

SHAMPOO Hindi *Champō* Massage and Hindi *Champā.*

The flowers of the plant *Michelia champaca*, which were once used to make scented hair oil. The word 'shampoo' entered the English language when in 1759 the Indian Vapour Baths were established in Brighton by the Bengali entrepreneur, Sake Dean Mahomed. His *champi* or 'shampooing' service, a therapeutic head massage, was so popular that a new title was created for him and he was appointed 'Shampooing Surgeon' to both George IV and William IV. To make the early formulations of what would later come to be known as *shampoo,* manufacturers would boil soap in water and add to it such plants as henna, aloe, jasmine, rose and musk, all of which were traditional Indian ingredients.

SHANGHAI Mandarin *Shang* On and *Hai* The sea.

China's largest city owes its prosperity to being a port but the other meaning of the word – to be shanghaied – meant to be press-ganged into joining the navy for a life on the sea.

SHANK'S PONY Frisian *Schanke* A Leg.

To ride on Shank's Pony is to walk, so there is no pony and instead you must use your legs. The word shank is used for anything relating to a leg such as lamb shank or anything that is long and thin such as the shank of a nail or an anchor. The tall Plantagenet King Edward I was nicknamed Longshanks.

SHARK Mayan (Central American) *Shoc* Fish.

The word is thought to have been brought to England by the explorer Sir John Hawkins (1532–1595) who exhibited a shark in London after returning from the Caribbean.

SHAWL Persian *Shal* A strip of cloth.

SHERIFF Old English *Scir* shire, a county as in Hampshire and *Reeve* An official appointed to keep the peace.

A reeve is one of the oldest democratically elected positions as he was a serf appointed by other serfs to keep order for the lord who owned both the land and those who worked it during feudal times. An early example of self regulation. Later the title was applied to law keepers responsible for whole counties or shires so they became shire reeves which became corrupted to sheriffs. *See also Alderman.*

SHERPA Tibetan *Shar* East and *Pa* Inhabitant.

Men from the mountains of Nepal (the women are called *Sherpinis*) have immense natural strength at high altitudes and are therefore frequently called upon to assist in mountaineering expeditions, notably up Mount Everest. The most famous Sherpa was Tenzing Norgay (1914–1986) who, with Edmund Hillary (1919–2008), reached the summit on 29 May 1953.

SHERRY A corruption of *Jerez*, in the Cádiz region of Spain, where sherry is produced. Any sherry produced outside of Cádiz must not be called S*herry, nor Jerez* or *Xérès*, unless it is clearly stated that it was produced elsewhere.

SHODDY Scraps of wool surplus to requirements in the weaving process and also recycled fabrics were called shoddy. Since this material invariably had shorter strands, the clothing made from it soon became dishevelled and the wearer was said to be shoddily dressed.

SHOULDER Anglo-Saxon *Scylan* To divide.
The shoulders are the point at which the arms divide from the body.

SHOULDER-BLADE German *Blatt* A leaf.
The derivation is an allusion to the bone's broad, flat surface.

SIERRA Spanish *Sierra* Saw.
The word is applied to mountain ranges such as the Sierra Nevada, on account of their jagged peaks' resemblance to the teeth of a saw.

SIESTA Spanish *Sesta* Sixth hour.
The midday nap takes place during the sixth hour of daylight.

SIN Latin *Sons* Guilty.

SINISTER Latin *Sinister* On the left side.
The Romans always entered the houses of friends with their

right foot first, because the left side of the body was associated with evil.

SIRLOIN French *Sur* Upon or above and *Longe* Loin.

This cut of meat is taken from below the ribs and above the loins. Samuel Johnson was the first to spell the word *Sirloin*, probably having been taken in by claims of King James I knighting a piece of meat. According to this folk etymology, while being entertained at Hoghton Tower near Blackburn, the king exclaimed, 'Bring hither the sirloin, for it is worthy of a more honourable post, being, as I may say, not sirloin, but Sir Loin – the noblest joint of all!'. In actuality, the word *surlonge* had entered the language during the reign of James's predecessor, Queen Elizabeth I.

SKEDADDLE Greek *Skedannumi* To retire tumultuously.

The word skedaddle originated in America, in the nineteenth century, to describe a hasty retreat.

SKI Old Norse *Skith* Snowshoe, length of wood.

Skiing is Scandinavian in origin only being introduced elsewhere for recreational purposes in the early twentieth century.

SKILL Old Norse *Skil* Discernment.

A person said to be skilful was one who could accurately distinguish between different things of a given class.

SKINFLINT In Old England, having walls made of flint blocks was a sign of affluence. In order to imitate it, poor people who were unable to afford whole blocks, would 'skin the flint', that is, face walls made of ordinary bricks with thinner pieces of flint. Hence people who were loath or unable to spend money were referred to as skinflints.

SKIP Norse *Skopa* To run.

    History does not relate why the usually ferocious Norsemen were inclined to run in this way.

SKIRT Norse *Skyrta* A shirt.

SKY Swedish *Sky* Cloud.

    Originally the word referred not to the upper atmosphere but to the cloud formations lower down.

SLAVE Old French *Esclave* Slav.

    The people of Slovenia were so frequently captured and enslaved by other Europeans that their name became synonymous with slavery.

SLEAZY Latvian *Silesian* From Silesia.

    The large area of central Europe known as Silesia was once noted for fine quality fabrics that were often shipped out of the Baltic ports of Latvia. When poor quality imitations began arriving the Latvians coined the derogatory term sleazy.

SMITH Saxon *Schmeid* Smite.

    A smith or blacksmith smites hot metal on an anvil with a hammer. The word was later used to describe any type of craftsman such as goldsmith, silversmith, tinsmith, locksmith and even wordsmith but smith on its own, or smithy, always refers to the original blacksmith or metal worker. Before the Norman Conquest, after which the French word *Carpentier* Carpenter was introduced for woodworkers, they were known as woodsmiths.

SNAIL Old English *Snaca* Snake, creeping thing.

    The term was also once used to describe slugs.

SNIP Anglo-Saxon *Snippe* or *Snibbe* The bill of a bird.
To snip something is to cut it with scissors, similar to the action of a bird's beak.

SNOB Latin S*ine Nobilitate* Without Nobility.
Those who were not of noble birth were listed in college registers as *s.nob*, an abbreviation of S*ine Nobilitate*. Thus it has become a label for anyone who strives to associate with those of a higher social class. *See also Nob.*

SNOOKER Derives from the military slang for a newly joined cadet. The game was invented by British officers stationed in India as an alternative to billiards.

SOCCER Abbreviation of *Association*, from Football Association (FA), in much the same way as Rugger is the slang term for rugby. *See also Cricket and Rugby.*

SOCIAL Latin *Socius* A companion.

SOFA Arabic *Suffa* A bench.

SOLDIER There are two possible derivations suggested for this word. One is that it comes from Latin *Sal dare* To give salt, since early Roman soldiers were certainly paid in salt as it was considered a scarce but essential part of their diet without which their health would be threatened. A more likely possibility however is that it comes from the *Solidus*, a solid gold coin first introduced by Emperor Diocletian in AD 301 with which soldiers were paid. *See also Salary.*

SOMBRERO Spanish *Sombra* Shade.
Hats with particularly wide rims much used to provide shade in sunny climates such as Mexico.

SOMERSAULT Old French *Sobresault* from Latin *Supra* Above and Latin *Saltus* A leap.

SOPRANO Latin *Supra* Above.
> The Soprano sings with a voice above all others.

SOUFFLÉ Latin *Sufflare* To blow.
> Food with air blown into it by being whisked into a froth.

SOUTH Germanic *Sunnon* Sun and the region of the sun. To northern European observers, the sun is always in the south of the sky. *See also North, East, and West.*

SOUTHPAW American. The term for a left-hander originated in baseball. Most pitches are arranged so that the batsman faces east thus avoiding the sun in his eyes during the afternoon when most games are played. The pitcher or bowler therefore faces west and if he is a left-hander, with the ball in his left hand or left paw, he holds it on the south side of his body. *See also Awkward and Gawky.*

SOVEREIGN Italian *Sovrano* Above and Latin *Regno* To govern.
> A sovereign is above the government. The term was first used to describe a gold coin by King Henry VII (reigned 1485–1509), due to its great size and importance.

SPAGHETTI Italian *Spago* A cord.
> Spago means a cord of any size, so spaghetti are tiny cords.

SPANIEL Spanish *Hispaniola* The West Indies, where this breed of dog originated.

SPHINX Greek *Sphingein* Bind.
> The mythological sphinx is a creature that is formed by

joining, or binding together, the body of a lion, the wings of a bird and usually the head of a woman.

SPIDER German *Spinne* To spin. Spiders spin webs. A cobweb is derived from Old English *Coppe* A Spider. *See also Spinster.*

SPINACH Arabic *Hispanach* The Spanish plant.
The first known mention of spinach is in Turner's *Herbal* of 1568, where it is described as 'a herb lately found and not much in use'.

SPINNEY Latin *Spina* A thorn.
A spinney is a small woodland very often with thorny shrubs and bushes.

SPINSTER German *Spinne* To spin.
It was once said that a young woman should never be married until she had spun herself a complete set of linens, for herself, for her table and for her bed. As a result, it was fairly common to see unmarried women spinning away. Hence, they were known as spinners or spinsters. *See also Spider.*

SPLENDID Latin *Splendeo* To shine.

SPRITZER German *Spritzen* To squirt.
A spritzer is a measure of wine and a squirt of soda water.

SPUTNIK Russian *Sputnik* Travelling companion.
The Russian satellite Sputnik 1, launched in 1957, was the first man-made object to orbit the earth.

SQUASH Narragansett (north-eastern North America around Rhode Island) *Ascutaquash* Pumpkin.
A North American plant with a particularly difficult name so

the early settlers renamed them squashes. It is unclear why they did not call them pumpkins as that word is European, being derived form the Greek *Peopon* Large Melon.

SQUIRREL Greek *Skiouros* Shadow-tailed.
Squirrels have large tails which they can use to shade the rest of their bodies when it gets hot.

STADIUM A Greek race-course of 607 feet (184 metres). The first to be built was at Olympia where the original Olympic Games were held.

STAGNANT Latin *Stagnum* A pond or pool.
Stagnation rarely occurs in bodies of water larger than ponds as there is more opportunity for movement.

STAIR Anglo-Saxon *Astigha* Mounting, climbing up.

STALACTITE Greek *Stalaktos* Dropping.
Stalactites are rock formations that 'drop down' from the ceilings of caverns. They are created by particles of rock held in the water that remain behind when the water drops from the ceiling. A stalagmite is the opposite formation, created by particles of rock still held in the water after it has dropped off the end of the stalactite down onto the floor where it slowly accumulates to form a pillar.

STAMPEDE Spanish *Estampida* A crush.
A stampede is a panic-stricken rush of animals or people that may well result in participants being crushed.

STARBOARD Old English *Styri* Rudder.
Before ships had fixed rudders they were steered with very large oars held over the stern of the ship. These tended to be

on the right side of the ship as that was most convenient for the majority of sailors who were right-handed. Port, the left side of the ship, is derived from the usual practice of docking in a port with that side of the ship alongside the quay, thereby ensuring that the steering oar on the starboard side was not crushed against the harbour wall. *See also Stern.*

STARCH Old English *Sterchan* To stiffen.

Starch is a thickening agent used in cooking, paper manufacturing and to stiffen formal clothes

STARVE Anglo-Saxon *Steorfan* To die, not necessarily from starvation.

Thus when Chaucer wrote in *Troilus and Cressida* about people starving he meant that they died but not from lack of food.

STEAK Norse *Steik* To roast.

STEEPLECHASE Horse races used to take place on unmarked courses between towns and with prominent church steeples very often marking the finishing point.

STEGOSAURUS Greek *Stego* Roof and *Saurus* Lizard.

This dinosaur is so named because of the bony plates that lined its spine and might be described as a 'roof' in the same way as a snail's shell might be viewed as its 'house'. *See also Dinosaur.*

STEP-FATHER Anglo-Saxon *Stoep* Bereaved.

The prefix *step-*, when applied to father, mother, son etc. reflects the probable cause of them being a relation at all.

STERLING A corruption of German *Easterling*.

A name given to money from the east of that country which was highly regarded for the purity of the metal used in the coins. Indeed, so poor was the quality of English money during the reign of Richard I that it was often stipulated that payments be made in *easterling*.

STERN (As in severe.) Old English *Austern* Austere.

STERN (As in the back of a ship.) Norse *Stjorn* Steering.
Ships are steered from the stern, or back. *See also Starboard.*

STET Latin *Stet* Let it stand.
The word is used when a correction is made that should not have been. Stet is an instruction to the printer to ignore the correction and let the typesetting stand as it once was.

STETHOSCOPE Greek *Stethos* Chest and *Skopeein* To examine.
Stethoscopes were invented in France in the nineteenth century to investigate conditions in the chest.

STEWARD Anglo-Saxon *Stiward,* from *Sti* A house and *Ward* A guardian as in a ward of court.

STIMULATE Latin *Stimulus* A goad or spur.
There was nothing like a spur to stimulate a horse into action.

STINK Anglo-Saxon *Stenc* Fragrance.
The word originally described pleasant aromas. Stench is form the same source.

STINGY Anglo-Saxon *Skinch* To give short measure or to squeeze out in driblets.

STIRRUP Old English *Stig* To mount and *Rap* A rope.
Stirrups, the means by which a rider mounts up into the

saddle, were originally fixed to either end of a rope across the horse's back. The earliest horsemen did not use stirrups but the invention proved crucial when horses were first used in warfare as they enabled the rider to turn in his saddle and fight without falling off. The derivation shows that to start with they were an aid to climbing into the saddle rather than a means of providing stability to the rider.

STOMACH Greek *Stomakhos* Gullet.

Tummy is a child's way of simplifying the word stomach.

STRANGLE Greek *Strangos* Twisted.

A twisted ligature is the most effective method of strangulation, whether a scarf as used by the Thugees or a mechanical garrote as used in executions. *See also Thug.*

STRATEGY Greek *Strategos* A general, from *Statos* Army and *Aegin* To lead.

STRING Latin *Stringo* To draw tight.

Stringent, meaning to adhere tightly to rules, is from the same root.

STYLE Latin *Stylus* A pencil.

The word style was originally applied only to the appearance and design of the written word such as would be created by a pencil.

SUBURB Latin *Sub* Under and *Urbs* City.

Rome was built on seven hills and the outskirts of the city, mainly outside the city wall, were therefore below the level or 'under' the central urban part of the city. *See also Palace.*

SUCCUMB Latin *Cumbere* To lie down.

> Giving way to overwhelming pressure invariably results in lying down, sometimes even to die.

SUEDE French *Suède* Sweden.

> The earliest trade route for the soft leather was from Sweden to France where it was used in the manufacture of gloves.

SUFFRAGE Latin *Suffragium* Voting tablet.

> In Rome votes were recorded on tablets of stone or wood. The process of voting is therefore closely connected to the tablet or *suffragium* so much so that the right to vote became known as suffrage. The term suffragette was coined in a disapproving English newspaper by feminising suffrage, the right to vote, with the feminine suffix 'ette'. But instead of the word remaining a derogatory expression as they had intended, it was adopted by the campaigners who achieved female suffrage in Britain in 1928.

SUGAR Entering the English language from Sanskrit *Sharkara*, through Persian and Arabic *Shakar*, through Italian *Zucchero* and French *Sucre*, the etymology of this word follows the proliferation of the commodity it describes and is a perfect example of a word's migratory habits through many languages before reaching English.

SUNDAY *See Days of the Week.*

SURLY Anglo-Saxon *Sur* Sour and *Lic* Like.

> From this we get sour-like, which was later contracted to surly.

SURRENDER French *Se rendre* To yield oneself.

SWAN Old English *Geswin* Singing bird.

> An illusion to the song, the swansong, that the birds are supposed to sing before death, an expression that now describes any final performance

SWASTIKA Sanskrit *Svasti* Well-being.

> The cross with arms turning at right angles to each other is one of the most ancient good luck symbols known to man, evidence of its use dating back to Neanderthal times. It features largely in Hindu and Buddhist cultures and was in use throughout Europe in flags, coats of arms and mosaic decoration until its adoption by the Nazi party when its popularity and usage understandably decreased. The title pages of books about India by Rudyard Kipling (1865–1936) were decorated with swastikas, not something that would have been done after 1939. *See also Nazi.*

SYNAGOGUE Greek *Syn* Together and *Agoge* Gathering.

> Originally called *Beth Keneseth* House of Assembly by the Hebrews, but was changed with the translation of the Old Testament into Greek.

SYNTAX Greek *Syn* Together and *Tassein* To arrange in order.

> Syntax is the structuring of words and language into correct sequences.

TABBY Arabic *Attabiya* A district of old Baghdad where a patterned silk with stripes similar to those of a tabby cat was made.

TABOO Tongan (Polynesian) *Tapu* Forbidden.
Captain Cook brought the word back to Britain after being impressed by the constraint that the inhabitants of Tonga, or The Friendly Islands as he named them, had to various practices and customs that had been declared taboo.

TACKY Archaic slang *Tackey* A small and therefore inferior horse. It now refers to any cheap and corny goods.

TANDEM Latin *Tandem* At length.
Originally referring to a carriage pulled by two horses going in single file, tied one behind the other and now mainly used to describe a bicycle made for two where the riders sit one behind the other. *See also Bicycle.*

TANTALISE From the Greek mythological tale of Tantalus who, afflicted with constant thirst, was submerged up to his chin in water and rendered unable to drink it. A tantalus is a case or stand for a collection of decanters, glass containers for wine or spirits.

TARAMASALATA Greek *Taramas* The salted roe of cod and *Salata* Salad.

TARANTULA This poisonous spider takes its name from *Taranto*, a port in southern Italy. Although they have now worked their way further north, at one time Tarantulas were relatively unknown in Europe being present only in the southernmost parts of the continent where they probably arrived on ships from Africa. It was believed in Dr. Johnson's time, and for a significant period afterwards, that the tarantula's bite could 'only be cured by music'. This cure is most likely to be related to the relaxation of the heart-rate that can be achieved by listening to soothing music which in turn limits the flow of poison in the bloodstream.

TARIFF Berber *Tariq ibn Ziyad* was a general in the Muslim army that conquered north Africa in 710AD and was then sent across the straits of Gibraltar to reconnoitre possibilities of invading Europe as well. He created a settlement in the southernmost point of Spain that was named Tarifa in his honour. Later in command of the Moorish army (Latin *Mauri* The tribe that inhabited the Roman province of Mauretania) he conquered most of Iberia. Tariffs were charges imposed at Tarifa on shipping passing through the Straits of Gibraltar. *See also Gibraltar and Morris Dancing.*

TARPAULIN A corruption of 'tarred palling'. A pall is a cloth covering for something such as a funeral pall which covers a coffin. A tarpaulin is a cloth covering which has been waterproofed with tar.

TATTOO Interestingly both senses of this word have a similar, onomatopoeic derivation. In the military sense the word is derived from Dutch *Tap-too* the drumbeat that called soldiers back to their barracks after the gin shops had closed. Later the word came to mean a gathering of troops for more sober activities such as marching to military bands. In its other sense, decorating the skin with ink, the word comes from Polynesian *Ta-ta-u* Hand colour, mimicking the repetitive tapping action of the hand in the application of ink. Tattoos in this latter sense were an indication of rank, as well as tokens of bravery and religious or personal devotion. The practice became popular in Europe after early explorers arrived home with tattoos they had acquired while visiting the Pacific Islands.

TAVERN   Latin *Taberna* A hut.
This word shares the same root as Latin *Tabernaculum* Tabernacle, the portable temple in which the Israelites carried the Ark of the Covenant.

TAWDRY   The word derives from St Audrey, or to give her proper name Etheldreda who was Abbess of Ely in the seventh century. Lace sold at a fair in Ely on St Audrey's Day fell out of fashion and was eventually considered tasteless, particularly by the Puritans who rejected all forms of adornment and gave it the derogatory name tawdry.

TAXI   Latin *Taxa* Charge and Greek *Metron* Measure.
A taximeter cab is a vehicle in which the charge is recorded by a measuring device. *See also Cab.*

TAXIDERMY   Greek *Taxis* An arrangement and *Derma* Skin.
Taxidermy is the skilful arranging and preservation of the skin of a dead animal.

TEEPEE   Lakota (Sioux) *Tipi* Dwelling.
A teepee is a conical tent constructed with poles and either

hide or canvas that could easily be moved as the nomadic North American tribes moved across the plains. A wigwam is a more solid construction with a thatched domed roof giving the appearance of an igloo and was erected for use over a longer period. *See also Igloo.*

TEETOTAL Total, with the initial letter doubled for emphasis. One who abstains absolutely from alcohol although its derivation suggests that it could also be used to describe any totality.

TELEPHONE Greek *Tele* Far and *Phone* Voice.
See also Cacophony.

TEMPERANCE Latin *Temperantia* Moderation.
Temperance is one of the four cardinal virtues, the others being Prudence, Justice and Courage. The Temperance movement, however, campaigned not for moderation in the consumption of alcohol but for its outright prohibition.

TERRIER Old French *Chien terrier* Earth dog.
A terrier is a small dog trained to flush foxes and badgers from their holes under ground.

TEXT Latin *Textum* To weave, as in to create.
Text is a group of words that have been woven into sentences.

THEATRE Greek *Theasthai* To view.
The theatre is now usually a place to see dramatic perform-ances but at one time it was a place to see anything. For example an operating theatre is a room where surgery takes place and medical students gather to view and to learn. *See also Audience.*

THIGH Anglo-Saxon *Theo* To swell.

 The thighs are the thickest or most swollen part of the leg.

THIMBLE A corruption of thumb bell, since the thumb was where sail makers wore them.

THRASHING When a father threatened to give his naughty son a good thrashing he was unconsciously alluding to threshing, the ancient practice of using a flail consisting of a hinged piece of wood to strike corn and remove the grain. *See also Threshold.*

THRESHOLD Old English *Therscold* To thresh.

 Threshing is the task of trampling cut corn to detach the grain from the straw. A threshold, the door way of a building, is likely to be trampled more than any other part of the house. The second meaning, a significant point, a new opening that ushers in a new start in a series of events such as in 'he was on the threshold of a great discovery', stems from the first.

THROMBOSIS Greek *Thrombosis* Curdling.

 Curdling is the process of thickening milk, the start of cheese making and other processes. A thrombosis is likewise a thickening of the blood that causes a clot.

THUG Hindi *Thag* Thief.

 The Thuggees were a network of thieves and bandits that preyed on travellers in India from the seventeenth to the nineteenth century. Hence the word *thug* entered the English language during the colonial era. *See also Strangle.*

THURSDAY *See Days of the Week.*

THYME Greek *Thyein* To burn a sacrifice.

 Thyme had great religious significance as well as being used for embalming, incense and a variety of medicinal purposes.

TIDDLY   Slang for slightly drunk.

TIDDLYWINK   Slang for an unlicensed public house, where the game was often played.

TINNITUS   Latin *Tinnire* To ring.
Tinnitus is a condition of the ear that artificially generates a constant ringing sensation.

TIP   Originally written on tipboxes as T.I.P., an acronym meaning To Insure Promptness.

TIPSTAFF   The attendant officer to a judge is so called because of his staff, which is tipped with a gold or silver crown.

TITHE   Old English *Teotha* A tenth part.
A tithe is a tax that requires one tenth of the produce grown by a tenant to be paid to the landlord who would then store it in a tithe barn. *See also Farm.*

TOAST   The practice of proposing a toast to someone's good health was originally restricted to that of beautiful or popular women. Bread that had been toasted and flavoured with spices was added to the wine, so that after raising a glass to the woman in question, it would seem as though her mere presence had improved its taste when sipped. The practice of clinking glasses together that often accompanies a toast derives from a much earlier, more discourteous time when, in order to put everyone at ease, Viking feasts would begin with the slamming together of goblets. The contents of one would splash and mingle with everyone else's thus sharing around any poison that had been added to a particular drink so it worked as a deterrent to prevent one man poisoning another.

TOBACCO Arawak (northern South American and Caribbean) *Tobago* Smoking pipe, rolled tobacco leaves.

Though credited with introducing tobacco from the New World, Sir Walter Raleigh was not the first to discover it. Almost a century earlier, Columbus named the island of Tobago after the plant, having been astonished to find people smoking there.

TOBOGGAN Algonquin (Central North America around the Great Lakes and eastern Canada) *Toboggan*. This was the language of tribes such as the Cree in modern day Canada.

A toboggan has a flat base with a curved front so that it rides with its full width over the snow. A sleigh or sledge, Norse *Sled* To slide, differs in that it has two runners.

TOIL Anglo-Saxon *Tilian* To till.

Tilling the ground with the primitive implements of the Anglo-Saxons must have been exceedingly hard work. Hence the adapted term is now applied to any arduous task.

TOMATO Nahuatl (Aztec) *Xitomatl* Plump thing with a belly-button.

The Spanish brought tomatoes to Europe and the first Englishman to cultivate the plant was John Gerard, author of *Gerard's Herbal* in 1597.

TOMB Greek *Tumbos* A burial mound under which were buried the ashes of a cremated corpse. The Latin *tumulus* is from the same root.

TORPEDO Latin *Torpere* To stun.

Electric eels belong to the order *Torpediniformes* and the naval weapons took their name from the species. In his dictionary Dr. Johnson noted that the 'fish while alive, if touched even with a long stick, benumbs the hand that so touches it, but when dead is eaten safely'.

TORTURE Latin *Tortum* To twist.
Twisting of body parts often played a part in the torture chamber and explains the word tortuous, clearly from the same root but meaning twisted, not torture.

TORY Gaelic *Tar a Ri* 'Come O King'.
The first Tories were the Irish supporters of the exiled King Charles II during the Cromwellian era. The cry was so frequently on their lips that it was adopted as the name for their movement.

TOWEL French *Touaille* Linen cloth.

TOWN Anglo-Saxon *Tune* A hedge or fence.
All early settlements were surrounded by defensive fortifications, meaning that the first thing visitors came across was a hedge or fence. Hence the word was given to the group of dwellings within. *See also Wall.*

TOXIC Greek *Toxikon* Poison used on arrows, from *Toxon* Arrow. *See also Arrowoot.*

TRASH Norwegian *Trask* Fine brushwood, such as the clippings of trees and hedges, too fine to be used for firewood.
Unscrupulous firewood traders would swell the size of their bundles by padding the middle with this worthless *trash*. Hence the word is used nowadays to describe anything deemed worthless, while in some parts of Britain the original meaning is preserved through *brash*, a combination of branch and trash, which is specifically applied to useless brushwood.

TRAUMA Greek *Trauma* A wound.

TREACHERY Norman English *Treacher* A traitor.

TREACLE Latin *Theriaca* Antidote to poison.

Treacle was originally a thick, syrupy medicine prepared as a treatment of snake bites. The word was also applied to the curative ingredients of water in what became known as spa towns. Springs or wells from which this water was obtained were called treacle wells made famous by Lewis Carroll's Dormouse in *Alice's Adventures in Wonderland* who claimed he had friends who lived in a treacle well but, by that time the medicinal origins had largely been forgotten, making it an absurd idea well suited to the story. *See also Dormouse.*

TREASURE Latin *Thesaurus* Storehouse.

A treasury is a storehouse for money and a thesaurus was a storehouse for any treasure. The popularity of Roget's *Thesaurus* has largely caused the word's meaning to be used exclusively for a storehouse of definitions, synonyms and antonyms.

TREK Africaans *Trekken* To haul.

This word was used by Dutch settlers in South Africa who undertook long arduous journeys from the coast inland to find farmland suitable for settlement. The terrain over which they travelled invariably meant they had to haul their carts manually.

TREMBLE Latin *Tremulus* To shake.

TRENCHER Old French *Trenchier* To cut.

In the Middle Ages, slabs of old bread that were thick and stale enough to cut on were often used instead as meat plates and they were called trenchers. After a meal, the used bread would then be given to peasants or dogs. Later the word described wooden platters on which whole meals were served without being changed between courses. A trencherman is one who is a heavy feeder and is probably not too concerned about how the food is served. A trench, a cut in the ground, derives from the same root. An example of one root providing two unconnected English words.

TRESS Greek *Trikhia* Rope.
A tress is a lock of hair that has been divided into three and braided so that it resembles rope. *See also Twine.*

TRIGGER Dutch *Trekken* To pull.

TRIM Old English *Trymman* Strengthen.
To trim a lamp or candle wick is to cut away unwanted and burnt sections in order to strengthen that which remains.

TROUSSEAU Old French *Truss* A Bundle.
A trousseau is the small bundle in which a bride carries her possessions to her new home after marriage. *See also Paraphernalia.*

TROUT Greek *Trogein* To nibble.
Though a perceptive glimpse of every fisherman's dream, the derivation actually comes from the grazing habits of the fish.

TRIVIAL Latin *Trivialis*, from *Tri* Three and *Via* Road.
Trivialis referred to a place where three or more roads meet and where people are likely to gather to discuss matters of little consequence.

TRUNK (As in an elephant's trunk.) Old English *Trump* as in trumpet since an elephant uses his trunk to trumpet. The

French retain *la trompe* but in English this has evolved into the less suitable trunk.

TRUTH Anglo-Saxon *Triewth* Faithfulness.

TSUNAMI Japanese *Tsu* Harbour and *Nami* Wave.
Enormous and destructive waves used to be called tidal waves but since it is now realised that they are not caused by tidal movements that name has lapsed. Tsunamis are caused by the displacement of sea water by earthquake or volcanic eruptions.

TUESDAY *See Days of the Week.*

TUMBLER A tumbler was a glass or other drinking vessel that had a rounded bottom which prevented the drinker from laying it down until he had drained the last drop. In other words they are glasses that tumble as they cannot stand upright.

TUNDRA Lapp *Tundar* Elevated wasteland.
The word refers to the permanently frozen subsoil of the Arctic regions.

TURKEY Early settlers in America wrongly identified the native bird as a guinea fowl believing it to be the same as the European Turkey, a type of guinea fowl, so-called because it was originally imported from Africa via Turkey. But the popularity of the American bird has resulted in it becoming the sole user of the name.

TURNCOAT This label for traitors originated from Savoy where the armies of the first duke considered it prudent to alternate their support between the French and the Spanish, both of whom had designs on his dukedom and could easily have overwhelmed him with superior forces. To successfully maintain this flux of allegiance, it was sometimes necessary for his troops to wear the blue uniforms of the Spanish and on other occasions the white ones of the French. The Duke therefore designed a coat with a different colour on either side that could be reversed, or turned, as it became politically prudent to do so.

TURNIP Anglo-Saxon *Næpe*.
A turnip is a neep, a Scots word for a root vegetable such as the swedes traditionally served with haggis and tatties on Burns night. The round shape of a turnip looks as though its has been turned on a lathe. *See also Parsnip.*

TURNPIKE The barriers on main roads where tolls were levied invariably consisted of a series of pikes on a pivot that could be swivelled, or turned, to open the road to a traveller who had paid his dues. Something similar is still seen at football stadiums and railway stations.

TURQUOISE French *Turquois* Turkish.
Though actually mined in the Middle East, in Iran and Sinai, this blue-green stone was named by Europeans after the Turkish bazaars at which it was purchased.

TUTTI-FRUTTI Italian *Tutti* All and *Frutti* The fruits.

TWENTY, THIRTY, ETC. The *-ty* suffix in these words is from the Anglo-Saxon *tig*, ten. Twenty is *twaintig*, two tens; thirty is *thritig*, three tens; forty is *feowertig* four tens, etc.

TWILIGHT Anglo-Saxon *Tweon* Between and *Leoht* Light.
Originally the word was *tween-light*.

TWINE Old English *Twin* Twin.

>   Twine is composed of two cords twisted together. Thread,
>   Old English *Thre* Three, on the other hand, signifies three
>   cords twisted together. *See also Tress.*

TYCOON Japanese *Taikun* Great lord, referring to the shogun or
>   commander-in-chief of the army. More recently the military
>   connection has been lost and it now refers to captains of
>   industry.

TYMPANUM Greek *Typtein* To strike.

>   Tympani are kettle drums in an orchestra, and the tympanic
>   membrane is the ear drum.

TYPHOON Mandarin *Tai* Great and *Fung* Wind.

>   Typhoons are tropical cyclones in the north-western Pacific.

UMBRELLA Latin *Umbella,* from *Umbra* Shade.

In the sunnier Mediterranean area umbrellas would have been used rather more to provide shade from the sun than for protection against the rain.

UMPIRE Old French *Non* Not and *Per* Pair.

An umpire is someone who is not paired with either party in a contest and is therefore able to provide an impartial verdict.

UNION JACK French *Jaque* A jacket.

The national flag of England, the St. George's red cross against a white background, was embroidered onto the coats of English infantrymen so that they could be identified in battle. This embroidered coat came to be known as the 'jack'. When Scotland and Wales united with England to form the British Isles, the jack was amended to include the colours of their flags and henceforth became known as the Union Jack.

URANUS Greek *Ouranos* Heaven and the God of Heaven.

The planet was first discovered by the British astronomer Sir William Herschel (1738–1822), and was named after him by the French, despite the fact that he himself had suggested naming it Georgius Sidus (George's Star) after his patron, King George III, in whose 'auspicious reign the star began to shine'.

URCHIN   Old English *Yrichon* Hedgehog.

Hence the spiny, globular sea creatures that resemble hedgehogs are called sea urchins. Young people who are unkempt, dishevelled and very likely with uncombed hair resemble hedgehogs and are also known as urchins.

URL   An acronym for *U*niform *R*esource *L*ocator, the term used to refer to a web address in general.

UTOPIA   Greek *Ou* not and *Topos* a place

A word thought to have been coined by Sir Thomas More (1478–1535) for use as the title of his book in which he described a perfect society in order to draw attention to the shortcomings in the current style of government. But of course this was not a place that could ever exist.

VACATION Latin *Vacare* Empty, at leisure.

Days that are empty of responsibility. *See also Vacuum.*

VACCINE Latin *Vacca* Cow.

A vaccine is a means of introducing a mild dose of a disease sufficient to induce immunity. Edward Jenner (1749–1823) noticed that milkmaids, who were constantly touching cows, did not suffer from smallpox but they did catch the far less virulent disease cowpox, and from this he deduced that the latter was producing immunity to the former. *See also Inoculate.*

VACUUM Latin *Vacare* Empty.

A vacuum is created when a vessel is emptied, even to the exclusion of air. *See also Vacation.*

VAGABOND Latin *Vagari* To wander.

Vagabonds and vagrants are impoverished people who invariably wander for lack of homes. *See also Extravagant.*

VALENTINE Little is known about St. Valentine but one theory claims that he secretly married young men to their lovers, having been forbidden from doing so by the Roman Emperor

Claudius II who believed that single young men made better soldiers. When his dissension was found out, St. Valentine was thrown in jail and on the night before his execution, he is reputed to have sent a note to his own beloved, signing off with that immortal cliché, 'From your Valentine'.

VALOUR Latin *Valere* To be strong.

VAMPIRE Magyar (Hungarian) *Vampir* Witch.

VANDAL The Vandals were a tribe from Germany who invaded the Roman empire and, most famously, sacked Rome in AD 455 showing their revulsion to the clean living and cultured inhabitants by wantonly destroying buildings and works of art. Since then the word has described anyone who deliberately destroys someone else's property.

VANILLA Spanish *Vainilla* Little pod.
Vanilla is a member of the orchid family. *See also Orchid.*

VARNISH Middle Latin *Vernix* Odorous resin, from Greek *Verenike*, from *Berenike*, the name of an ancient Egyptian Queen, and the Libyan city named in her honour (modern day Benghazi). The city is credited as the location of the first use of varnish.

VASECTOMY Latin *Vas* Tube or vessel and *Ectomy* Excsion, removal by cutting.
An appendectomy is the removal by cutting of the appendix.

VELLUM Old French and Norman *Veel, veau* Calf.
Vellum refers to a type of fine parchment that was made from the skin of a calf. It has the same root as veal.

VENISON Latin *Venare* To hunt. Latin *Ventionem* A hunt.
Venison was the meat obtained by hunting and originally referred to any meat of large game, such as deer or boar. *See also Humble Pie.*

VENTRILOQUISM Latin *Venter* Stomach and *Loqui* To Speak.
A ventriloquist entertains his audience by deceiving them into believing that his voice is coming from his dummy and not from his own mouth. To achieve this he must not move his lips and instead he must speak from further down inside his body.

VERGER A verge is a staff carried as a mark of authority. The verger of a cathedral carries the mace, or verge, of the dean.

VERMICELLI Latin *Vermiculus* A little worm.
An allusion to the worm-like appearance of this delicate pasta.

VERMIN Latin *Vermis* A worm.
The first creatures to be described as vermin were worm-like larvae that infested food. Now it describes any animal that becomes a nuisance whether a worm or something far larger like a mouse or a rat.

VERMOUTH German *Wermuth* Wormwood.
Antonio Bendetto Carpano, the Italian inventor of vermouth, was inspired by a German wine containing wormwood. Hence he honoured the herb by naming his new concoction after it.

VERTEBRA Latin *Vertere* To turn.
The vertebral column was considered the hinge of the body.

VEST Latin *Vestis* A gown.

Samuel Pepys wrote that King Charles II popularised the simple sleeveless garment to teach the nobility to be thrifty. *See also Vestry.*

VESTRY Latin *Vestarium* A room attached to a church used by the priest for storing his vestments. *See also Vest.*

VIGNETTE Latin *Vinea* Vine.

Small decorative paintings. The first capital letters of ancient manuscripts were so called on account of them being ornamented with flourishes reminiscent of vine branches.

VIKING Anglo-Saxon *Wicing* A pirate.

Vikings derived their name from *viks,* or coastal inlets, in which they hid. The element *vik* appears in many Icelandic coastal place names, such as Reykjavik, Húsavík and Keflavik, as well as one town simply called Vik.

VINEGAR French *Vin* Wine and *Aigre* Sour or rough.
See also Eager.

VISCOUNT The title of 'count' was given to a nobleman entrusted with the administration of a county. His deputy was therefore referred to as a 'vice count', which was reduced to viscount. In Britain counts are now called earls, from the Norse *Jarl* Chieftain, but their wives are still called countesses.

VISCOUS Latin *Viscum* Mistletoe.

A sticky viscous glue-like substance called birdlime was made from mistletoe to be spread on branches to catch birds. The word was later applied to any sticky substance.

VITAMIN Latin *Vita* Life and *Amine* Containing amino acids.

The word was coined as Vitamine in 1912 by Polish biochemist Casimir Funk (1884–1967), however upon discovering that vitamins did not in fact contain amino acids, the 'e' was dropped and the term became vitamin.

VODKA   Russian *Vodit* To dilute with water.
The spirit, often used in pharmaceuticals, was also known as the 'vodka of bread wine', a diluted version of a spirit made from grain.

VOLCANO   Latin *Vulcan* The Roman god of fire, forges and volcanoes. The equivalent god in Greek mythology is Hephaestus.

VOLUME   Latin *Volumen*, from *Volvo* To roll.
Before books were bound with pages, ancient volumes were simply long, narrow strips of parchment or papyrus that were rolled up when not in use. *See also Book and Vellum.*

VOYAGE   Latin *Via* A way and *Ago* To pursue.
A voyage once described a journey by land as well as by sea. This meaning has been preserved in the French language, as in the phrase '*Bon Voyage*', to bid farewell and good luck to someone embarking on a journey whether it be on land or sea.

VULGAR   Latin *Vulgaris* Common.
The original meaning did not signify something objectionable, but something that was ordinary. Vulgar Latin, for instance, was simply the dialect that was most commonly spoken.

WAGE Middle English from Old Norman *Wage* Pledge.

An employer pledges to pay a wage when work is completed. *See also Salary.*

WAIFS AND STRAYS Anglo-Norman *Waif* Ownerless property and *Estrayer* Stray livestock.

This expression is now normally applied to abandoned children, or people with very slender, child-like bodies, however the origin of these words shows that this was not always so. A waif was a stolen object that had been abandoned by the thief, whereas a stray was a domesticated animal that had strayed from its owner's premises. Waifs and strays became the property of the Crown until rightful ownership had been satisfactorily proved.

WAIST Old English *Waest* Growth.

So-called, perhaps, because this is where one's body is most likely to expand.

WAKE (As in a funeral gathering.) Old English *Wacu* Watch, as in guard.

The wake, originally the period before a funeral, is when the deceased is guarded or watched over in their home. Now invariably and inaccurately used to describe a gathering after the burial when it is no longer possible to watch over the deceased.

WALL Latin *Vallum* A rampart.
Cities were once surrounded by rampart fortifications for defence against invasion. The most usual form of rampart was a stone wall. *See also Town.*

WALNUT A corruption of Gall- or Wall-nut; the nut of Gaul, or France. *Gallia* and *Wallia* were interchangeable in reference to the country.

WALRUS Old Norse *Hrosshvalr* Horse-whale.
This entered into Old English as *Horschvael*, which has been reversed to *vael-Horsch* and corrupted to *walrus*. *See also Hippopotamus.*

WAR German *Werra* To quarrel.

WATERSHED German *Scheide* To divide.
A watershed is the divide between the catchment areas of two river systems.

WAVER Old Norse *Vafra* To flicker as a candle flame.

WEDNESDAY *See Days of the Week.*

WEED Old English *Woed* A herb.
What a turnaround, from a herb, the icing on the culinary cake, to the popular derogatory definition of a weed which is a plant in the wrong place.

WELCOME Anglo-Saxon *Wil* Well and *Coma* Someone who comes. *Wilcoma* was only used to welcome visitors who were gladly or well received. It was never applied to objects or concepts such as a welcome gift.

WELD A corruption of *Welled,* from *Well* To boil.
Welding involves heating metal until it 'boils' when it can be fixed to other pieces in a similar state.

WELLINGTONS The long waterproof boots were not invented by the Duke of Wellington but he did popularise them, being rarely seen without a pair. When mounted, he wore a pair with the back removed at the top for comfort when his knees were bent.

WENCH Old English *Wenchel* Child and *Wancol* Fickle, weak.
Now applied only to a young woman whose weakness has led to loose morals.

WEST Latin *Vesper* Evening.
The sun sets in the west. Vespers is the evening service held as the sun sets. *See also North, East and South.*

WHIPPERSNAPPER This term was applied in the seventeenth century to young loiterers on street corners who were often to be seen idly passing the time by snapping whips. Whip snappers were therefore lazy young men who lacked ambition. They may well have been distracting attention to enable a robbery to go unnoticed. *See also Racketeer.*

WHISK Anglo-Saxon *Fleder wisch* Feather broom made from a dried goose wing.

WHISKY, WHISKEY Irish *Uisge-beatha* Water of life. Latin *Aqua Vitæ* and French *Eau de vie* both mean precisely the same thing.

WHORE Norse *Hore* Adulteress.

WICKED Old English *Wicca* Wizard.

Wizards are now generally considered somewhat comical participants in Halloween festivities but at one time, when people were not quite sure if they really did have magical powers, they were undoubtedly feared and in all probability frequently also wicked.

WICKER Middle English *Wiker* Willow and Old Norse *Veikr* Weak.

On its own a branch of willow is spindly and weak but this makes it ideal for weaving into basketwork.

WIDOW Latin *Vidua* Bereft of a husband.

WILDEBEEST Dutch *Wilde* Wild and *Beest* Ox.

Otherwise known as the gnu, a kind of antelope.

WILL Old English *Willa* Determination.

A will is a declaration of a determination of what is to happen after death.

WINDFALL When the Navy built ships of wood, and at a time when timber was becoming scarce due to excessive felling, a law was passed to prevent people from chopping down trees that might be used for shipbuilding. The only exception was that they could make use of the timber if the tree fell due to storm damage and was therefore a 'wind fall'. Since these occurrences could not be planned they, and later any unexpected piece of good fortune, have become known as windfalls.

WINDOW Old Norse *Vind* Wind and *Auga* Eye.

The window allows us to see outside; it is our eye to the wind.

WINTER Norse *Wetr* Water.

Perhaps the climatic condition most noticeable in the English winter.

WITCH Old English *Wicce*, female form of *Wicca* A man who practices witchcraft. From German *Wicken* To conjure.

WOMAN Old English *Wamb* Womb.

An undeniable reference to femininity that shows that the 'man' part of the word woman has a quite different root to the word man.

WORLD Old English *Woruld* Human affairs, all humankind.

World means everything, the complete experience of humankind not just the planet we inhabit. Hence we say that farmers are in the farming world, and to describe a gathering of everyone, that the world and his wife were there.

WORM Norse *Waurms* Serpent.

It seems inconceivable that the humble earthworm could ever have been thought to be menacing yet it was. In Old English it was a *Wyrm* Dragon.

WREATH Old English *Writhan* To writhe.

The derivation is due to the method of construction of the wreath, as opposed to the tormented behaviour of mourners at a funeral where wreathes would have been found. Wreathes are made by twisting and turning branches and flowers in a writhing motion.

WRECK Scandinavian *Wrek* To wreak.

There are few situations in which more havoc is wreaked than when a ship is wrecked.

XENOPHOBIA Greek *Xenos* Foreigner and *Phobos* Fear.
Xenophobia is a fear of people from other countries.

XMAS Despite the traditionalist insistence on spelling Christmas
in full, the substitution of X for Christ has been around since
before 1100AD. It is the first letter of Christ's name when
spelt in Greek.

XYLOPHONE Greek *Xylon* Wood and *Phone* Voice.

YAHOO In *Gulliver's Travels* by Jonathan Swift, Lemuel Gulliver visits the Country of the Houyhnhnms where horses are the rulers and Yahoos are described as brutes in human form. Hence it is also applied to a crude, brash, uncultured person. The founders of the internet services company were apparently aware of the origin.

YANKEE *Janke*, a common Dutch surname, was a term used to describe Dutch-speaking colonists in America, generally in the north-eastern states. Eventually it came to refer to English-speaking colonists as well and to residents of New England with English ancestry in particular. Hence the Confederates of the south applied it derisively during the American Civil War, presumably as an allusion to their enemies' un-American provenance.

YEAST Sanskrit *Yasyati* To boil or bubble.
The expanding froth created when yeast is activated in the baking and fermenting process resembles the movement of water when it boils. Yeast is the oldest domesticated organism having been used in the preparation of food and drink for 5000 years.

YELL German *Gellen* To sing.

Not a very complimentary transition to the shrieking and shouting that we mean when we use the word today.

YNGLING Norwegian *Yngling* Youngster.

The *yngling* is a type of sailing boat that is a cross between a dinghy and a small keel boat that is now a class in Olympic yachting. It is so called because the designer, Jan Linge, built one for his young son.

YOKEL A yokel was a rustic who yoked oxen or other working animals.

YOLK Anglo-Saxon *Gealow* Yellow and the yolk of an egg.

In Anglo-Saxon, the letters G and Y were frequently interchanged, resulting in the adaptation of *gealow* to our yellow, which in turn was contracted to *yelk* and eventually corrupted to yolk.

YO-YO Tagalog (Philippines) *Yo-Yo* Come-Come which perfectly describes the actions of a yo-yo as it repeatedly climbs back up its string.

YUCK An expression of disgust for something that is onomatopoeic for the action of vomiting.

YULE Old Norman *Jol* A twelve day midwinter pagan feast, later adopted by Christianity. We still burn yule logs as part of the season's festivities.

ZIP CODE American *Zoning Improvement Plan*
The USA postcode.

ZOMBIE Kongo (A Bantu language spoken in present day Congo and Angola) *Zombi*, from *Jumbie* Ghost.
The word travelled across the Atlantic with the slave trade. In voodoo, a zombie is a dead person who has been resurrected and enslaved, or else a living person who has been given the 'zombie drug', which simulates death. The most famous case of the latter is that of the Haitian Clarvius Narcisse, who in 1962 was poisoned by a *bokor*, or sorcerer, with naturally occurring neurotoxins, then 'resurrected' and regularly given doses of the hallucinogenic plant *Datura*. Along with many others he was forced to labour in a trance on the bokor's sugar plantation until 1964 when his master died and the supply of the hallucinogen ran out.

ZOO Greek *Zoion* Animal.
The study and exhibition of animals in Zoological Gardens.

ZULU Zulu *Amazulu* The People of Heaven.